RESTORING A FALLEN CHRISTIAN

Rebuilding Lives for the Cause of Christ

GREG S. BAKER

www.GregSBaker.com

Restoring a Fallen Christian

Rebuilding Lives for the Cause of Christ

by

Greg S. Baker

Other Books by Greg S. Baker

Christian and Christian Living

Fitly Spoken – Developing Effective Communication and Social Skills

Restoring a Fallen Christian – Rebuilding Lives for the Cause of Christ

The Great Tribulation and the Day of the Lord: Reconciling the Premillennial Approach to Revelation

The Gospel of Manhood According to Dad – A Young Man's Guide to Becoming a Man

Rediscovering the Character of Manhood – A Young Man's Guide to Building Integrity

Stressin' Over Stress – Six Ways to Handle Stress

Biblical Fiction Novels

The Davidic Chronicles

Anointed

Valiant

Fugitive

Delivered

King

Adventure/Fantasy Novels

Isle of the Phoenix Novels

The Phoenix Quest

In the Dragon's Shadow

Phoenix Flame

Rise of the Dragon Spawn

More to come…

www.GregSBaker.com

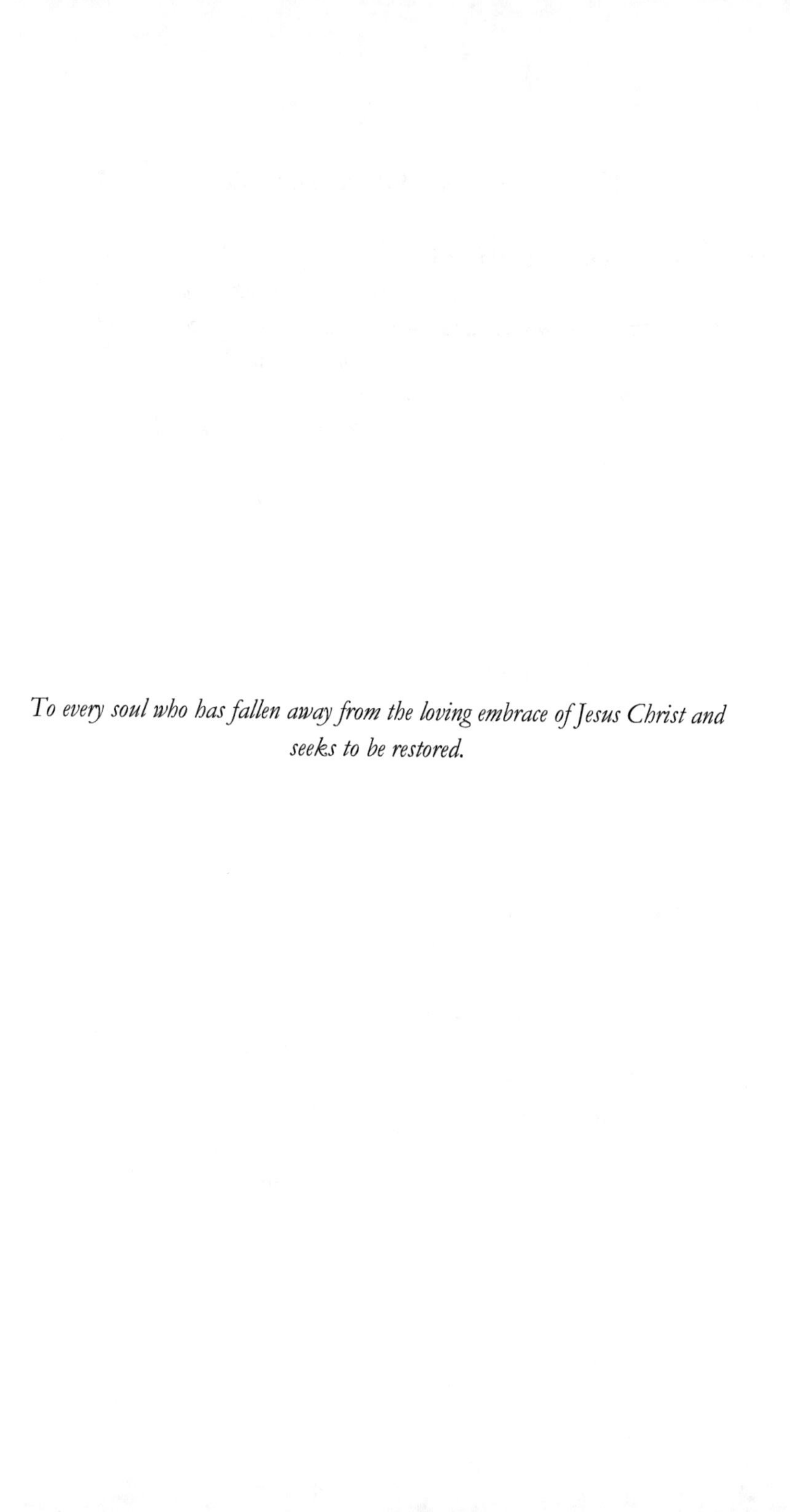

To every soul who has fallen away from the loving embrace of Jesus Christ and seeks to be restored.

Author's Note

The Bible records the falls of many men of God. I believe that each Christian that falls will in some way resemble these men. Each fell in a different way and for different reasons. The study of their issues and situations will go a long way in helping you to restore a fellow Christian who has fallen.

Look through these chapters and find where your friend or loved one is described at the beginning of the chapter, then read through it to gain an understanding of what you can do to restore him or her back to the grace, love, and peace of the arms of Jesus Christ.

Although it is doubtful that a fallen Christian will choose to read this book, I seek, nonetheless, to let such a one know that he is still loved, that Jesus still loves him, and that I, his fellow brother in Christ, still loves him.

And to those of you who seek to restore a Fallen Christian back to the loving embrace of Jesus Christ, thank you. Thank you for your love, patience, and dedication. Who knows how greatly the cause of Christ may be benefited by restoring a Fallen Christian back to Christ!

www.GregSBaker.com

Contents

1

Introduction

Having been in Christian circles all my life, I've come to observe a rather disturbing pattern among churches and Christian circles. We spend time, money, energy, and devotion in reaching the lost for Jesus Christ—as it ought to be—but then we ostracize, otherwise ignore, gossip about, defame, and generally drive away a Christian who has fallen or backslidden.

The Problem

This phenomenon first became very evident to me in Bible college. I'd watch sold-out young Christians prayerfully and sincerely venture into the dregs of society to pull out a drunken bum, give him the Gospel, clean him up, and bring him to church. This same wonderful Christian would then spit at the feet of a fellow Bible college student because the other student fell a bit in his Christian walk with God.

We obey the Great Commission, but then we ignore the biblical command to restore a fellow Christian when he falls.

> ***Galatians 6:1*** *– Brethren, if a man be overtaken in a fault, ye which are spiritual, restore such an one in the spirit of meekness; considering thyself, lest thou also be tempted.*

There really isn't a good reason for our failure in this area. In fact, if the truth be known, I believe we've hindered the Great Commission. How many more people could have been reached with the Gospel by those fallen Christians, if we took the time to restore them back to fellowship with God? How many great men and women of God were lost to us, because when someone fell, there wasn't a Christian to help restore him? What great soul winner, Sunday School teacher, pastor, missionary, or deacon did we lose because a spiritual Christian couldn't be bothered to restore a Fallen Christian?

The word "restore" is found only 17 times in the New Testament. The Greek word *"katartizo"* is translated a variety of ways, such as perfect, make, mending, fitted, framed, joined, prepared, together, and of course, restore. The imagery that is conjured to mind by just these few words is clearly that of bringing back someone who has strayed, mending that which is torn, fitting something broken back together, and joining back together again that which was separated.

The Fallen Christian needs more than an open door in order to come back. There is healing that must take place—forgiveness of self and of wrongs done to him must be accomplished. Mending and careful preparation must be done before the Fallen Christian can be restored.

Too often, a Fallen Christian is left alone to try and glue back the pieces of a shattered life. This is not the way Jesus intended it to be. I have been in Christian work for over twenty years. I pastored a church for thirteen of those years. In all that time, I learned one significant truth: everyone falls at some point and to some degree. Therefore, everyone needs a Restorer.

The Purpose of This Book

The purpose of this book is to help you restore a Fallen Christian in the spirit that the Bible suggests—meekness. The Scriptures already provide various solutions and methods for restoring a fallen or backslidden Christian. We will be examining these methods and solutions in order to equip the Restorer (the spiritual Christian) to help bring back those who have fallen away.

Not everyone falls the same way. Truth be told, most of us are currently backslidden somewhere in our Christian life. We are all susceptible to the wiles of the Devil. We are all sinners and we all struggle to keep our minds and spirits in Christ Jesus all the time.

The methods of restoration vary from person to person and from type to type. It is impossible to stereotype any particular fallen Christian. Indeed, to do so would very much be like a doctor who diagnoses every runny nose as a cold. You can't do that and have much success. Yet all fallen Christians possess certain characteristics that can be identified and then dealt with. It is the job of the Restorer to recognize these characteristics and then equip himself with the knowledge, wisdom, and power to restore them back to the Christian fold. It is his job to labor in prayer, to beseech God on the Fallen Christian's behalf, and prepare himself to aid in the restoration process.

This book is written to equip the Restorer to restore a Fallen Christian. Fallen Christians who read this book can be helped, and there is no doubt that some who read this have fallen away and may very well be seeking a means to be restored. However, the vast majority who read this book know someone, love someone, or are close to someone who has fallen away from the love of Jesus Christ. It is these Christians who are seeking some means—any means—to help them come back.

This book is for you.

PART ONE

Identifying and Helping to Restore the Fallen

Goals and Purpose of This Part of the Book

There are many different ways for a person to fall or backslide. It is important for the Restorer to be able to identify why someone fell so that you know how to help restore them. Without this understanding, you very well might be the proverbial bull in a china shop. The damage you can do, even with all the good intentions in the world, is enormous.

Nevertheless, the command to restore the Fallen is given to us.

The following chapters are to equip the Restorer with the following objectives:

1. To understand his or her role as a Restorer.
2. To be able to identify the different types of Fallen Christians.
3. To isolate the most common factors that contribute to a Fallen Christian's current emotional and spiritual state.
4. To gain insight into how a Fallen Christian might be restored.
5. To gain the tools and wisdom necessary to put yourself in the best position to help restore the Fallen Christian.

Once you have equipped yourself with the knowledge of how to restore a Fallen Christian, there are two more things you will need that no one can really teach you: compassion and mercy. Demonstrate these two qualities, or else you will fall to your own pride.

Finding the Help and Resources You Need

Each chapter in this section of the book—other than the first chapter which focuses on the Restorer only—is broken into specific sections to aid you in finding the information and guidance you need. These sections include:

1. Characteristics and Signs of This Fallen Type
2. Why the Person Under Consideration Fell
3. Outward Signs to Look For

4.   How to Restore This Type of Fallen Christian
5.   A Word to This Fallen Christian

The *first section* gives you a basic list of characteristics that often typify a believer who has fallen in a similar manner as the biblical example under consideration. These signs, if you will, will help you to quickly identify what type of Fallen Christian you are dealing with. In other words, if you find similar signs of the one you are trying to restore to those listed in this section, then you may want to read that particular chapter carefully, since many of the things your friend is facing are also the things the biblical example faced.

The *second section* gives more detail of what led up to the fall of the biblical example. Knowing why a person falls is important in determining what you can do to help restore him. Much like a doctor, until a proper diagnosis is made, a remedy can't be prescribed.

The *third section* gives a greater and more detailed list of the visible signs that accompany someone who has fallen in a manner as the biblical example under consideration. Use this list to gain a fuller understanding of what such a Fallen Christian may be going through and experiencing.

The *fourth section* gives step-by-step instructions as to what you can do and how to do it. Follow these biblical principles to help restore a Fallen Christian back to the loving embrace of Jesus Christ.

The *fifth section* addresses that type of Fallen Christian directly. This section is meant to bring hope to someone who has fallen, as well as give you the proper perspective in dealing with that particular type of Fallen Christian.

2

The Restorer

The key to restoration is the Restorer. In essence, a Restorer is a guide to help a fellow Christian find his way again spiritually, to rediscover the love of Christ, and to be accepted back into the fellowship of other believers.

Galatians 6:2 – *Bear ye one another's burdens, and so fulfill the law of Christ.*

2 Timothy 2:24–26 – *And the servant of the Lord must not strive; but be gentle unto all men, apt to teach, patient, 25 In meekness instructing those that oppose themselves; if God peradventure will give them repentance to the acknowledging of the truth; 26 And that they may recover themselves out of the snare of the devil, who are taken captive by him at his will.*

Ecclesiastes 4:9–10 – *Two are better than one; because they have a good reward for their labour. For if they fall, the one will lift up his fellow: but woe to him that is alone when he falleth; for he hath not another to help him up.*

> ***James 5:16*** *— Confess your faults one to another, and pray one for another, that ye may be healed. The effectual fervent prayer of a righteous man availeth much.*

Most people when they fall don't need someone to point out the obvious. They know all about their fallen state. They are perfectly aware of their sin. They don't need to be kicked or walked over. They need a hand up. They need someone to help them.

In fact, it is part of our job as a Christian to become a Restorer. Someone who has strayed from the spiritual way, from their biblical roots, will have a difficult time coming back. It may not be because they don't want to come back, but because they don't think they can.

The Greatest Hindrance to the Restoration Process

The greatest hindrance to a Fallen Christian's restoration is usually fellow Christians. One of the most common concerns I hear from people who used to go to church and who are now thinking of returning is some variation of, "Will I be judged for what I've done?"

Christian arrogance and superiority has driven more people out the doors of our churches than almost anything else I can think of. Christians who criticize the failings of others, who gloat over the mistakes of others, and who refuse to sully themselves with the consequences of another's sin make it difficult and sometimes impossible for one of God's children to be restored to the faith.

When our tongues are used to flay the spirit of our fellow brethren or when our actions radiate rejection and disinterest, the Fallen Christian is led to believe that they can't return—and worse, no one desires their return.

This attitude, I believe, is a direct result of two things:

1. A fear of the Christian to biblically consider himself.
2. A misunderstanding of certain Scriptural references regarding disassociation with certain types of believers.

Taking the first point, it is often easier for a Christian to attack a fault and then distance himself from a Fallen Christian because he doesn't have to face his own penchant to commit sin. It is an act of misconstrued comparison. We use other Christian's failings to bolster our own reputation in the eyes of others. If we aren't as bad as so and so, then we can feel good about ourselves. We feel we can ignore our own sin since our sin isn't as bad as so and so.

I've discovered that someone who is often the most vocal about condemning sin and the sinner alike is someone who is probably trying to hide from the fact they are just as likely to commit the same sin. It is an attempt to hide a weakness within themselves and a fear of facing that weakness.

> **Galatians 6:1** – *Brethren, if a man be overtaken in a fault, ye which are spiritual, restore such an one in the spirit of meekness; considering thyself, lest thou also be tempted.*

The Bible clearly commands the Restorer to consider himself. To look within and realize he is just as likely to fall, just as likely to sin as the one whom he wishes to restore. The realization of this truth helps the Restorer approach the Fallen in a true spirit of meekness. If you try to help someone any other way, it will come off wrong. You'll do more harm than good.

Now let's examine some of the verses that are often misunderstood. The following Scripture verses have been used over and over by Christians as justification of condemnation, alienation, and rejection of a Fallen Christian. A closer look at them may reveal, however, a different perspective.

1 CORINTHIANS 5:11

> **1 Corinthians 5:11** – *But now I have written unto you not to keep company, if any man that is called a brother be a fornicator, or covetous, or an idolater, or a railer, or a drunkard, or an extortioner; with such an one no not to eat.*

To begin with, the word "company" is talking of mixing together in a casual sense, to associate in a way we would normally think of when we attend a party or social gathering of some sort. This is borne out by the last phrase of the verse, "…with such an one no not to eat."

The Scriptures teach that we should avoid being casual about someone's sin. This doesn't mean that we can't try to restore them. In fact, this entire passage deals with a man who Paul asked to be removed from the church, but later, in 2 Corinthians 2:7, these same Christians were commanded to forgive and comfort this same Fallen Christian. They were commanded to restore him.

I don't care who it is. I won't go to the bar to associate with anyone—Christian or otherwise. A bar is the wrong setting for any Christian and should be avoided for casual gatherings. But I will invite this person to church—again, no matter who it is, what they have done, or their current spiritual state. I'll love this person. I'll even sit with him in church and invite him to my house for lunch.

Yes! To eat with him! The difference is that I am controlling the atmosphere. We are not going out on the town for a casual night of fun and revelry. He is at my house so that I can demonstrate the love of Christ to him and hopefully restore him back. Remember this: Whoever controls the atmosphere controls the influence.

Where I may invite a Fallen Christian to my house in order to be a blessing to him, I won't go to his party where he controls the music, the food, the drink, the friends, the company, the place—and thus the influence. No, in order to influence someone, you must be in control of the environment.

Who does the most influencing at your church? Your pastor does. He controls the music, the preaching, the singing, and the teaching. He does the influencing. In such an environment, you will have more power as the Restorer.

You can help restore a Fallen Christian without having to immerse yourself in his sin. You don't have to be a drunk to reach a drunk. You don't have to be a fornicator to reach a fornicator. But you do need compassion to make a difference. Although I may avoid a casual atmosphere I cannot control and any situation that condones or encourages sin, I will seek to bring a Fallen Christian into an environment I control in order to help him.

2 THESSALONIANS 3:6, 14

2 Thessalonians 3:6 – Now we command you, brethren, in the name of our Lord Jesus Christ, that ye withdraw yourselves from every brother that walketh disorderly, and not after the tradition which he received of us.

2 Thessalonians 3:14 – And if any man obey not our word by this epistle, note that man, and have no company with him, that he may be ashamed.

The purpose of the passage is a warning not to follow and thus get caught up in the disorderly conduct of those who become busybodies. Certainly these people are fallen, and following them is not a proper means of restoring them back to the faith. These people are more than just fallen. They are attempting to become the dominant force within their sphere of influence. They seek to take charge and control things to the point of ignoring the Word of God as warned in verse 14.

But if you take a look at verse 14, we learn what we hope to gain by this withdrawal from them: to cause these Fallen Christians to be ashamed. The Greek word translated "ashamed" conveys the idea of realizing the existence of proper reverence. These Christians were so caught up in themselves they weren't giving Jesus or His chosen man the proper reverence. If they can come to a point where they are ashamed by it, they can be restored.

The withdrawal from their influence was an attempt to get them to realize the error of their ways and to come back. Not to ostracize them and ignore them.

But the key to the passage is actually found in verse 15:

> *2 Thessalonians 3:15* — *Yet count him not as an enemy, but admonish him as a brother.*

Ah, here then is the heart of the matter. We aren't supposed to treat these people as if they're suddenly enemies of the faith, but rather to treat them as a brother with the full intention of bringing them back to the faith.

2 TIMOTHY 3:1–5

> *2 Timothy 3:1–5* — *This know also, that in the last days perilous times shall come. For men shall be lovers of their own selves, covetous, boasters, proud, blasphemers, disobedient to parents, unthankful, unholy, Without natural affection, trucebreakers, false accusers, incontinent, fierce, despisers of those that are good, Traitors, heady, highminded, lovers of pleasures more than lovers of God; Having a form of godliness, but denying the power thereof: from such turn away.*

I believe this is talking about a type of Christian that has not just fallen but turned away from the truth and then perverted it in their hearts. These people can't be restored because they don't want to be restored. Besides the language of verses 2–5, look at the following comments made of these people:

1. They actively sought to turn away others from the truth (verse 6).
2. They are ever learning but always seeming to not quite get the truth (verse 7).
3. They intentionally resist the truth (verse 8).
4. They have corrupted their minds (verse 8).
5. They have become reprobate concerning the faith (verse 8).

There are some Fallen Christians that just won't be restored due to their own mindset. They have literally become enemies of the cross. As such, you should avoid them. If they ever indicate a willingness to return, then your interaction with them should change. But what should never change is the fact that you love them and that they are in your prayers constantly.

One of the following chapters discusses this topic in length to help the Restorer understand that there are some that cannot be restored. This is not to say they can't come back to God. They can. It's just that you won't be able to persuade them to return. It'll have to be something between them and God.

2 JOHN 1:10, ROMANS 16:16–17, and 1 TIMOTHY 6:3–5

2 John 1:10 – If there come any unto you, and bring not this doctrine, receive him not into your house, neither bid him God speed:

Romans 16:17–18 – Now I beseech you, brethren, mark them which cause divisions and offences contrary to the doctrine which ye have learned; and avoid them. 18 For they that are such serve not our Lord Jesus Christ, but their own belly; and by good words and fair speeches deceive the hearts of the simple.

1 Timothy 6:3–5 – If any man teach otherwise, and consent not to wholesome words, even the words of our Lord Jesus Christ, and to the doctrine which is according to godliness; 4 He is proud, knowing nothing, but doting about questions and strifes of words, whereof cometh envy, strife, railings, evil surmisings, 5 Perverse disputings of men of corrupt minds, and destitute of the truth, supposing that gain is godliness: from such withdraw thyself.

I believe these passages are talking about false prophets and teachers—those who intentionally, or even ignorantly, promote false doctrine. It is due to these verses that I won't let anyone teaching something contrary to the Scriptures into my house, be it another religion or a parody of Christianity. Nor will I join with them in some benign endeavor. They are coming to my door to promote their false beliefs. I won't receive them, and I dead sure won't ask God to bless their endeavors. Thus, I won't even work with them in something where people could learn of or become enamored with their false beliefs.

These passages have nothing to do with a Christian who has gone wayward and wishes to return. This is about those who try to use God, Christianity, and the Scriptures for their own ends or who seek to spread a perverted truth. The Bible is clear on how to treat such people under those circumstances.

To be clear, the teaching does not encourage you to be rude or to vilify them. We are commanded to love even our enemies. The command in these verses is to avoid being caught up in their false teachings.

MATTHEW 18:15–17

Matthew 18:15–17 – Moreover if thy brother shall trespass against thee, go and tell him his fault between thee and him alone: if he shall hear thee, thou hast gained thy brother. But if he will not hear thee, then take with thee one or two more, that in the mouth of two or three witnesses every word may be established. And if he shall neglect to hear them, tell it unto the church: but if he neglect to hear the church, let him be unto thee as an heathen man and a publican.

This passage isn't just talking about a Fallen Christian either. Rather, it is talking about how one Christian ought to address a grievance with another Christian. Either or both Christians involved may or may not be fallen. This is about two Christians finding resolution over their differences in an earthly matter. Lord willing, the process will never go so far as to being forced to bring in the entire church to deal with such a relationship problem.

The teaching focuses on the reconciliation as paramount—even over getting your way. Never does our Lord wish for Christians to simply cut off another Christian without some effort at reconciliation. You might be angry—justifiably so even—but that is not sufficient to treat a fellow Christian wrongly. There are to be at least three major efforts at reconciliation before cutting them off from your life.

This is not to say that failure to reconcile with them gives you permission to hold a grudge and refuse to forgive them. Neither does it say to cut them off forever. Just a few verses later, Peter comes to Jesus with a question of forgiving someone who hurts him. Jesus responded that forgiveness isn't something you keep a record of, but rather it is something that ought to become an instinctual and integral part of our daily life.

But honestly, if a Christian is so fallen that they aren't willing to listen to anyone, then they can't be brought back anyway. They clearly don't want to be brought back. But the effort of trying to reconcile them is still important. Once all efforts have failed, you can still continue to lift them up in prayer.

The Right Attitude for the Restorer

In order to help someone back, you must have the right attitude first. In many instances, the person who is in the best position to restore a fellow Christian is often the one who has been hurt the worst by the other's fall. Thus it takes quite a bit of maturity to achieve the correct attitude.

The Scriptures mention three things that must be done:

1. Meekness
2. Self-consideration
3. Bearing another's burdens

The second often leads into the first, which then enables the third. Put another way, an honest look at your own heart will always cause you to realize you are just as wicked, just as sinful, just as decadent as the fellow who was overtaken in a fault. Knowing this, you will approach them with meekness (an intentional restraint of power), thus enabling you to help shoulder their burdens and cares.

Without these ingredients, you'll be unable to restore a fellow Christian to the fellowship of the Spirit and of our Lord Jesus Christ.

Of course, love and prayer are important factors. Without them, I wouldn't even attempt it. In fact, you could say the attempt to restore someone is evidence of your love and your love is evidence of your prayer life. But without the proper attitude, your love will not accomplish what you wish it to. Many loving people have said the wrong thing at the wrong time to the wrong person and created a mess.

So let's break these down, shall we?

Self-Consideration of the Restorer

It is a natural extension of our sin nature to feel superior to those who have fallen. We look at a backslider and we justify our own actions with a statement such as, "Well, at least I'm not that bad!" Or even: "I'd never do something like that!" Or how about: "I knew it! I could see it coming a mile away!" Then we turn up our noses and turn our backs, because there is no way that we'd dare allow ourselves be associated with someone who's done what they have done!

As I've already stated, we fear looking into our own hearts lest we discover that we too are just as capable of such sin. But we are! That's the point God is trying to make here. Anyone is capable of any sin if the circumstances, people, and place were just right. And I mean any sin from murder to child molestation.

You say, "Not me!" Ah, then perhaps you aren't aware of what God thinks about that:

> ***Jeremiah 17:9*** *– The heart is deceitful above all things, and desperately wicked: who can know it?*

Indeed, who can know it? You can't. God can. He searches the heart, does He not? And yet you are so convinced of your own incapability to commit a particular sin. That is the problem. Once you believe you are incapable of something, you've deceived yourself and have made it so that you can't help others.

It is the knowledge of "There but for the grace of God go I!" that we achieve the proper mindset to help others.

> ***1 Corinthians 10:12*** *– Wherefore let him that thinketh he standeth take heed lest he fall.*
>
> ***Proverbs 16:18*** *– Pride goeth before destruction, and an haughty spirit before a fall.*

The Scriptures have much to say on this. Beware of your pride. All of us are capable. It is this knowledge that allows us to look upon the Fallen and feel compassion for them and to allow our hearts the correct attitude to help them. It is when we know we're capable that we set safeguards and rules in our lives in an effort to avoid temptation. If you don't, you will leave yourself vulnerable to temptations in those areas.

Meekness of the Restorer

We tend to equate meekness with timidity, which is inaccurate. The Scriptures teach us that Moses was the meekest man in the whole earth (Numbers 12:3), yet no one would dare say he was timid—quite the contrary. So what is meekness?

A good biblical definition of meekness would be the restraint of power. Other words that could be used to define it would be "gentleness" or "mildness." Can an infant, just having learned to crawl, be gentle with his 200-pound father when they wrestle? Not really. As hard as the infant tries, he can't hurt the 200-pound dad.

But the dad, on the other hand, must be gentle with his son lest he inadvertently hurt him. This restraint of power on the dad's part is meekness.

We have so much potential to cause further hurt to a Fallen Christian. They messed up, and we chew them out, ignore them, are rude to them, turn our backs on them, and generally disregard them. This only causes the Fallen Christian further pain and spiritual damage.

It's true; you might be able to say, "I told you so." Just don't. You might be right and they wrong. You don't need to rub it in. They've probably figured it out by now anyway. How damaging is it for a person not to find the love, tenderness, forgiveness, and care of fellow Christians when they fall? Job said it best when his three so-called friends spent so much time accusing him:

> ***Job 16:2*** *– I have heard many such things: miserable comforters are ye all.*

I agree. If you don't show some restraint of your superior and arrogant position, you're a miserable comforter as well.

The Restorer Is to Bear Another's Burdens

Here is Galatians 6:1 along with verse 2:

> ***Galatians 6:1–2*** *– Brethren, if a man be overtaken in a fault, ye which are spiritual, restore such an one in the spirit of meekness; considering thyself, lest thou also be tempted. Bear ye one another's burdens, and so fulfil the law of Christ.*

Bear ye one another's burdens. That's the command. It is the law of Christ. Interestingly enough, verse 5 seems a direct contradiction.

> ***Galatians 6:5*** *– For every man shall bear his own burden.*

It isn't. The Greek word "bear" is the same in both verses, but the Greek word "burden" is not. In verse 2, the word "burden" is that of carrying a weight. In verse 5, the word denotes a burden of service—or specifically, a duty tasked (see verse 4).

Although every one of us has a task we must do for the Lord—one that no one else could or can do for us, the weight of life—the burden of sin is something we can help people carry. In fact, it is something we ought to, as Christians, help carry.

Interestingly enough, the more time you spend helping others carry their burdens, the more your own become lighter and easier to carry. This is just the way it works. People who carry the greatest weight of guilt, sin, and life are those who are more self-centered. If you are focused on others, your own weight is significantly decreased—which, by the way, enables you to be more efficient in the task or service God has called you to do.

__Hebrews 12:1__ – Wherefore seeing we also are compassed about with so great a cloud of witnesses, let us lay aside every weight, and the sin which doth so easily beset us, and let us run with patience the race that is set before us.

Caring for people's cares is what is meant by bearing the burdens of others. We try to relieve just enough weight so they can get above water and breathe, just enough so they can regroup, just enough to allow them to see the path back.

It's worth it.

Illustrations of the Restoration Process

Years ago, a couple began attending the church I pastored. They were related to another family in the congregation and had moved into town to be closer to family. The husband had an alcohol problem. In fact, after they'd first moved into town, he spent over $10,000 on booze in the space of two months.

His wife called me after a Sunday night service. "He's at the bar," she told me. I could hear the distress in her voice.

"Do you know which one?" I asked.

She told me and then asked if I would go get him and bring him home. I obliged—somehow thinking I was embarking on an adventure. It was only the second time I'd ever been in a bar—the first was to preach a sermon for a preaching class assignment in Bible college. When I walked in, several other people recognized right away that I didn't belong there. I could see them snickering and whispering and I overheard several rude comments. After all, I walked in wearing a suit and carrying a Bible. They knew I shouldn't be there.

The man I sought sat slumped on a bar stool facing a huge mirror that ran the length of the bar. He had a beer in front of him and had quite obviously been there for some time.

I slipped up behind him and just stood there silently, waiting for him to notice me in the mirror. After a few moments—and more snickering and snide comments from some other drunk patrons— he looked up. The instant he did and spotted me in the mirror, his face completely drained of any color. He spun around and stared at me like I was some phantom come to haunt him. He swallowed visibly and asked, "Preacher, what're you doing here?"

"I've come for you," I said, ignoring even more comments from the other denizens. "Come on, it's time to go home."

Very meekly, he followed me out the door and to my car. I drove him home, speaking gently to him, not chiding, nor lecturing, just telling him that he can have victory over his alcohol in Jesus.

We began to meet every morning at the church for Bible study and prayer. We were able to restore this man to fellowship with Jesus Christ, and he now pastors a church out East. God is good.

Another man heavily involved in our church, a soul winner and a strong believer, slipped and fell into drugs. I remember how devastated he felt and looked. He was so embarrassed, so distressed over his failure. It was troubling because he was such a role model for children in our church. Kids loved him. But this? What should we do? Well, we didn't beat him up, cast him out of the church, stomp all over him, or make a public spectacle of him.

No, we picked him up, brushed him off, got him the help he needed, and then loved him back into the fellowship of the Spirit. He is now a faithful church member, active in many aspects of the Lord's work, and actively winning souls to Christ on nearly a daily basis. Will he ever go back to drugs? I doubt it, but no matter if he does, we should seek to restore him.

Here are two examples of men who fell but were loved back into the fold. Hundreds, if not thousands, of souls are on their way to Heaven because a group of church members took it upon themselves to restore fellow Christians, instead of condemning them and tossing them out of the church. These restored Christians then went out and spread the good news of a loving and merciful God!

If you're going to be successful as a Restorer for the Lord Jesus Christ, you'll need to get your attitude right. It's amazing what God can do if we allow ourselves to become the vessels of God's use.

In the following chapters, we will be examining different types of Fallen Christians as well as describe the Scriptural methods for restoring them. Here is a list of the ten types of Fallen Christians we will be reviewing:

1. **Peter** – Fell because of failure and depression.

2. **King Saul** – Fell because he sought to do the right things in the wrong ways. He allowed difficult circumstances to make exceptions to the rules.

3. **The Prodigal Son** – Fell because he believed the world could provide him with happiness.

4. **Judas Iscariot** – Fell (per se) because he had a secret sin, an addiction, that he never dealt with and he allowed it to rule his thinking and actions.

5. **King David** – Fell because he let his guard down and allowed a fit of passion to lead him into sin.

6. **King Solomon** – Fell because he allowed the wrong influences too close to his heart.

7. **Cain** – Fell because he felt cheated and slighted by God.

8. **Jonah** – Fell because he disliked God's will and didn't think it was right.

9. **Absalom** – Fell because he allowed hatred and bitterness to consume him.

10. **King Nebuchadnezzar** – Fell due to pride, putting himself in God's place.

11. **Samson** – Fell because he was a fool, carelessly following the path of least resistance with complete disregard for **consequences.**

12. **The Apostate's Fall (Hebrews 6:4–8)** – Fell intentionally by rejecting the teaching and truths of Jesus Christ in his life—apostasy.

Not everyone can be restored, but all can come back. The thoughts and methods described below are biblically sound. I think you'll find that about every person you know who is fallen will have one or more of the qualities in the above list.

If you know that your friend or loved one, let's say, fell because he let his guard down and allowed a fit of passion to lead him into sin, then you need to read and study the chapter on King David. The Scriptural truths that applied to restoring David will also apply to your friend or loved one.

You may also find that a Fallen Christian embodies several aspects of those listed above. In this case, study the corresponding chapters and see how they can help you restore such a Christian back to the loving fold of Jesus Christ.

3

Peter's Fall – Failure and Depression

Text to Study: John 21:12–17

Characteristics and Signs of This Fallen Type

1. Feels like a failure.
2. Couldn't live up to his own, someone else's, or his understanding of God's expectations.
3. Wants to run away from the responsibilities of the Christian life, because he feels he may repeat his failure.
4. Desires to return to his old lifestyle simply because it is the only other thing he knows.
5. Can be restored fairly easily with a little bit of love and patience.

Why Did Peter Fall?

In John 21:12–17, we have the story of Peter's meltdown and decision to quit the ministry and return to his old life. But why? I believe his decision to run had to do with what had happened at the cross. Peter had denied Jesus three times. Peter felt like a failure and didn't deserve to be called a disciple of Jesus Christ.

It began back in the upper room, before Jesus was betrayed. Peter said in Luke 22:33, "Lord, I am ready to go with thee, both into prison, and to death." I believe Peter meant that, too. In fact, I know he did. When the mob came to arrest Jesus, Peter demonstrated his willingness to die and go to prison by taking up a sword and attacking the servant of the high priest (John 18:10).

Peter succeeded only in cutting off the ear of this servant, but not because that was his intention. Peter was a fisherman by trade, not a soldier. Either the servant moved or Peter missed, but his aim was to kill or wound the servant in an effort to drive the mob away from Jesus Christ. He sought to be Jesus' deliverer, His savior so to speak.

Jesus did something then that confused and confounded Peter. First, Jesus rebuked Peter in Matthew 26:52 by saying, "All they that take the sword shall perish with the sword." Jesus than healed the servant's ear.

I believe this was what tore Peter apart and confused him. He tried to stand up for Jesus. He risked death and imprisonment, and Jesus just told him to stop being a fool and put away his foolish sword before he foolishly hurt someone. It is possible Peter had his entire foundation of expectations ripped right out from underneath him. Peter had tried to do what he thought was right. He had tried to make good on his promise in the upper room and got rebuked!

I don't think Jesus was trying to hurt Peter, but Peter's exuberance was built on entirely misconstrued principles. Jesus didn't need a soldier to defend Him. Jesus didn't need a deliverer or savior. Jesus needed to go to the cross. Jesus needed to die there, and Peter's efforts worked against that purpose. However, Peter hadn't come to accept that yet.

So here is Peter. His efforts had been rebuked. The rest of the disciples were fleeing. The angry mob had taken Jesus. What should he do? He was now completely unsure of himself, his actions, his feelings, and any direction he thought to take. He did what all of us do under similar circumstances. He ran. Not far, just far enough to follow surreptitiously from a distance.

He still doesn't know what to do. He can't intervene—Jesus already rejected such action. He can't petition for Jesus' release—that would most likely land him in jail too. Unsure, confused, he finds himself near a fire someone lit to stay warm on a chilly night perhaps. He stretches out his hands and one of the men there, seeing him, suddenly asks, "Art thou also one of His disciples?" Taken off guard, having no plan of action, he denies it! Twice more he denies it, even to the point of cursing. Everything that he said he would not do, he just did. His confusion, insecurity, and possibly hurt feelings cause him to fall.

The Scriptures tell us that Peter went out and wept bitterly (Matthew 26:75). He's ashamed of himself. Everyone knows of his failure, his false boast, and his denial. For the next three days until Jesus rose from the dead, he would most likely be the one who sulked the time away. Even after Jesus rose from the dead, he felt like he couldn't do it anymore. He felt like he couldn't serve his Lord anymore. He quit. He went fishing.

Not because he hated Jesus, but because he figured Jesus didn't want anything to do with such a failure.

Outward Signs to Look For

There are several outwards signs you can look for to determine if the Fallen Christian you are wanting to help restore is someone much like Peter.

1. *Depression.*

2. *Feelings of unworthiness and failure.*

3. *Will retreat from church, the Bible, and prayer.*

4. *Will not reject God, Jesus, or the Bible. They will even claim a love for them but may feel unworthy of them.*

5. *Will probably have unrealistic or high expectations of what it means to live the Christian life.*

6. *Will often compare themselves to other Christians.*

7. *They will often retreat to something they know or knew before their Christian life.* This will often be something familiar to them, something they understand or feel they understand.

8. *Will have difficulty facing former Christian friends.*

9. *Will begin, justly or unjustly, to consider themselves an outsider and believe other Christians are either judging them continuously or no longer love them.*

10. *In some cases, feelings of being unfit for church or Christianity will abound.* They may even convince themselves that being absent from church is best for everyone else too.

This is perhaps one of the most common types of fallen states for a Christian. How many people do we know who tried to live up to some personal expectations of Christian living, only to fail and quit altogether? There are many Christians who no longer attend church because they failed to live the Christian life.

If this type of Fallen Christian is left alone too long, they will begin to justify their position in an effort to come to some form of stability in their life, even to the point of developing a hatred and antagonism toward all things Christian. It is an attempt to patch up a wounded spirit.

In my office, I've often heard phrases like this: "I blew it. I messed everything up. I've ruined everything. It's all my fault." And they're right. They did blow it. What they need to see is how much God loves them and how easy it is to come back to Him. They need to know that their fellow brethren in Christ will also accept them back.

Few Christians ever plan to fail. Those who become leaders, or who obtain a reputation in Christian circles or within their own church, take failure more seriously than do others. It is often devastating to their psychology. It becomes hard to face followers, peers, and other leaders.

How to Restore This Type of Fallen Christian

Actually, the restoration process here is fairly simple and often easily done—if done soon enough. The real danger here is waiting too long and giving the Fallen Christian the chance to justify his actions, to spin events into his own favor, to reconstruct his memories into something he feels he can live with.

Once things get to that point, it becomes much, much harder to restore him.

Here is the process outlined:

Step 1: Pray for the Fallen Christian

Everything begins and ends with prayer. Before you launch out to restore this person, pray for wisdom and guidance. Make sure you are being directed by the Lord. Getting yourself in the right frame of mind always begins with bathing the Fallen Christian in prayer first.

Step 2: Go to the Fallen Christian

This person rarely seeks out strong Christians to discuss his failure because it means reliving the failure. Most people don't like doing that. Someone needs to go to him. That's what Jesus did for Peter. He went to Peter in John 21:4.

Examples abound to demonstrate how vital this is. Hurt and injured people just don't very often try to restore themselves after what they consider to be a fairly major failure. They will hide, refuse to come to church, refuse to call, and refuse to attend church functions. This leads to a cycle of self-stigma. Because they withdraw from people who love them, they no longer feel loved. This then reinforces their reasoning for withdrawing in the first place, which just makes them feel even less loved. It is a vicious and deadly cycle.

Nip that in the bud right away. Go to them. Call them. Show up at their house. Don't wait for an invitation—and don't wait too long.

Step 3: Set a Calm, Caring Atmosphere

Jesus cared for Peter. Jesus even cooked dinner to make sure everyone was relaxed and at ease. This gave Peter time to lower his defenses. Jesus didn't launch right into the problem. His very presence spoke volumes, so He just tried to set Peter at ease first.

When you approach someone who has backslidden or fallen away, and they know you know, they will be defensive and on guard against any perceived attack or innuendo. They expect you to be upset. They expect a harsh lecture. They expect disapproval and condemnation.

Set them at ease first. I make it a goal to get them to laugh with me three times before we ever even approach the subject of their backslidden state. I try to include them in my life by sharing something funny or a mistake I recently made. This helps to set them at ease.

Once this is done, try to get them to bring the forbidden subject up by acting genuinely confused about their recent absence. Let me give you an example of an encounter with a teenage girl who, after making a mistake, fell away from church.

After setting her at ease, I said, "We've really missed you around church. I didn't do anything to offend you, did I?"

"Oh no!" she protested. "That's not it at all."

"Really? You just don't like me then?"

"No!" She looked at me in concern. "You know. It's what I did. That's all."

I frowned. "What you did? You don't think we care about you?"

"No! I just feel embarrassed. I don't know what people will think of me."

I continued to look confused. "How have those that do know acted towards you? Did they hate you or love you?"

A pause. "I guess they love me."

"Then I'm confused. What is there to worry about? We want you to come back. In fact, I insist. Our church can't love you like we want to if you aren't around."

She showed up the next Sunday. Notice how, without saying so, I implied that I didn't think she liked me because of her absence. This is something that never would have dawned on her before. Jesus used this technique on Peter when He asked, "Lovest thou me?" From there it was fairly easy to demonstrate that I cared not only about her, but about her recovery. I showed I was more interested in her getting back on her feet than I was about a mistake neither she nor I could change.

Step 4: Try Reasoning with the Fallen Christian

As I will show, many Fallen Christians can't be reasoned with. But this type can be. Jesus pointed at the fish—the very object Peter had been so hard at work trying to catch… and failing—and asked, "Lovest thou me more than these?" Three times Jesus tried to show Peter that serving Him wasn't about his success or failure, it was about his love for the Saviour. Once Peter understood this, he went out not too long afterward and preached that great sermon at Pentecost, where 3,000 people were saved and baptized.

Show him the illogic of this thinking. Build a verbal logic trap that forces him to rethink his decisions. Remind him of key verses that force him to realize that failure is only failure if he quits.

With the teenage girl mentioned above, I simply reasoned her out of every objection and fear she possessed. I showed her the only real fear was fear itself. I asked her how her current solution to the problem—hiding from everyone—actually helped her. I then taught her how facing those same fears would actually dispel them, but hiding from them only reinforced her fears. We went from hiding from church to attending church the next Sunday.

Step 5: Don't Compare Him to Another Christian

Don't let him do it to himself either! Peter made the mistake of wondering what Jesus had in mind for John. Jesus replied in John 21:23, "What is that to thee?" Jesus' plan for Peter was unique and special. Jesus refused to allow Peter to rob himself of that plan by comparing himself to another.

Don't let a backslidden Christian compare himself to another Christian. Remind him that his service for the Lord is unique and different than what the Lord has in mind for anyone else. As long as he is trying to make comparisons, he will continue to be ineffectual. You must show him that God's will for another has no bearing on him or his ability to do God's will.

Follow these four simple steps and you'll succeed in bringing many Christians back into the fold. Done with love and the right attitude, the success rate for restoring this type of Fallen Christian to fellowship with God is high.

Many of the Fallen Christians I deal with fall under this category. They are easily won back to the Lord because they never left the Lord; they just felt isolated from Him. The Devil loves to remind us of our failings, he loves to rub our noses in it, even remind us of Scriptural references that seem to condemn us. Satan is an expert at condemnation. He is the accuser of the brethren who delights in reminding us of our failings.

We must remind a person like this that Jesus isn't in the condemning business. We must remember those words spoken by Jesus to the woman taken in the act of adultery: "Neither do I condemn thee: go, and sin no more" (John 8:11).

A Word to This Type of Fallen Christian

It would be naïve to assume that only Restorers will read this book. Although this book is written for the Restorer, let me pause here to say something to the Fallen Christian who feels that he or she fits within this category.

Your guilt is a good sign. I would be more nervous for a Christian who messes up and is not even bothered about it than I am for you. The journey of your life is not defined by the mistakes you make, but by how you chose to live with those mistakes. Running, hiding, and ignoring God and your fellow Christians will serve only to allow the mistake and sin to dominate and rule your life.

It's true—not every Christian will understand or even forgive you. But I would rather live with the knowledge of the few who don't than live wondering if anyone does. You handle your mistake not by hiding it, but by admitting it and then growing beyond it. The Bible tells us to confess our faults one to another (James 5:16). This is more than the flu you seek healing from, but your difficulties and besetting sins that are dominating your life.

It is amazing how admitting a fault to a fellow Christian actually creates the desire in them to love and help you. Their acceptance is important to your healing from feelings of guilt and rejection. But when you seek to hide your sin from everyone, people still pick up stray feelings that something isn't right. People wonder what you are trying to hide and then wonder why you are trying to hide it. This will in turn give you the impression of rejection.

Some of my strongest and most loyal church members are those who once sat in my office and said, "If I tell you what I did, you will hate me and kick me out of the church." I didn't and have yet to, and now they serve God greatly! So can you.

4

King Saul's Fall – Justified Mistakes

Text to Study: 1 Samuel 13:8–12, 15:21–30, 26:21

Characteristics and Signs of This Fallen Type

1. Allows difficult situations to make exceptions to doing the right thing.
2. Justifies his actions to deflect feelings of guilt and sin.
3. Constantly tries to do right in wrong ways.
4. Is much more difficult to restore due to his inability to admit his fallen state.
5. Sees himself as more a victim than a sinner.

Why Did King Saul Fall?

Saul's downfall began when he tried to do right things in wrong ways (1 Samuel 3:8–13). His failure to abide strictly by God's commands and laws caused God to reject him from his kingship (1 Samuel 13:13–14) and, very possibly, from the lineage of the Messiah as well. God gave both to David.

And it's not as if Saul was a vile or wicked man—at first. Eventually, he did vile things in desperation and rage. But Saul got caught up in what many Christians get caught up in. When things begin to get difficult, the difficulties, the circumstances, the problems became an excuse to violate the law of God, to disregard the will of God and do things your own way.

Saul feared an upcoming battle. Outnumbered, perhaps, with poorly trained troops, poor armor, and poorer weapons, he faced a trained military army arrayed in the latest battle gear set to destroy him. He knew that a sacrifice to the Lord would help, but Samuel—a Levite and able to perform the sacrifice—was late. Scared and thinking that if he didn't do something fast, he and his men would all die, he offered the sacrifice himself. This was a mistake—a sin! Only a Levite could offer sacrifices to the Lord. Saul was from the tribe of Benjamin and thus forbidden to perform priestly duties. When Samuel did show up and demanded an explanation for this violation of God's law, Saul gave this excuse:

> ***1 Samuel 13:12*** *– "Therefore said I, The Philistines will come down now upon me to Gilgal, and I have not made supplication unto the LORD: I forced myself therefore, and offered a burnt offering."*

Notice the phrase, "forced myself." He used the desperate circumstances to justify his sin. This is something that he did over and over again until finally God removed him altogether.

He did it again when he disobeyed God's commandment to destroy the Amalekites (1 Samuel 15:3). When asked why he had disobeyed the command, he responded this way:

> ***1 Samuel 15:20–21*** *– "Yea, I have obeyed the voice of the LORD, and have gone the way which the LORD sent me, and have brought Agag the king of Amalek, and have utterly destroyed the Amalekites. But the people took of the spoil, sheep and oxen, the chief of the things which should*

> *have been utterly destroyed, to sacrifice unto the LORD thy*
> *God in Gilgal."*

Notice how he shifts blame to the people. Notice how he explains to Samuel that circumstances conspired against him and he had no choice. When chastised about it, he says this in verse 24: "I feared the people, and obeyed their voice."

His fixated hatred and jealousy of David resulted from David's willingness to do what Saul should have done, but did not because of the difficult circumstances. David killed Goliath. That was something Saul should have done, but everyone else feared this monster of a man and no one but a boy rose to the challenge. But the women of Israel began to sing in 1 Samuel 18:7 that "Saul hath slain his thousands, and David his ten thousands." This ate away at Saul's heart until he became homicidal and sought to destroy David.

Saul's pursuance of justification for wrong actions led to his downfall. In this, he is not alone. Many Christians follow a similar path and head towards a spiritual fall.

Outward Signs to Look For

This type of Fallen Christian is also very common. If pressed, I'd have to say that this one and the Peter type are the two most common types of Fallen Christians.

Jesus even spoke of this type of Fallen Christian in the Parable of the Sower (Matthew 13:21), where tribulation caused the Christian to fall away and become unfruitful. Here are some of the outward signs of this type of Fallen Christian:

1. *Will justify sin by using circumstances and problems as excuses.*

2. *Will be quick to say that the problems gave him no choice.*

3. *Will admit his sin (1 Samuel 15:24) but will pass it off as an unfortunate result of circumstances beyond his control.*

4. *Will take the easy road and believes that his difficult circumstances justify it.*

5. *Will retain some of the trappings of Christianity because he believes that the outward appearance is important (1 Samuel 15:30).* This person will often come to church, bring his Bible, say "Amen!" during the preaching, and generally look like a good Christian.

6. *Will often seek to discredit Christians who are doing things the right way even during difficult circumstances.* Like Saul who hated David, this Fallen Christian will seek to level the playing field by cutting down fellow believers to build himself up. It is easy to justify a sin when everyone else is also willing to do it.

How to Restore This Type of Fallen Christian

Doing so is possible, but difficult. The following steps will help you to help such a Christian back to where they can get right with God.

Step 1: Pray for Him

Waltzing in to fix things without first having prayed long and hard for this individual may do more damage than good. You will need tremendous wisdom to reach this type of Fallen Christian. So pray first. I would even recommend spending a significant amount of time praying and fasting.

Step 2: Prepare for a Long and Arduous Process

This Fallen Christian is extremely difficult to restore. It can be done, but not without a lot of work. David eventually helped Saul see reason, but not after many, many years of running from him.

People who justify wrong actions can only do so by erecting a wall of false reason that somehow makes sense only to them. Tearing down that wall is not easy. It is defensive in nature. Tearing it down will reveal weakness, insecurity, and injured pride. Most people who are unwilling to face these truths will resist such attempts.

Usually, it takes a trusted authority figure to break down these walls. A good friend may do it, if the friend also fills a role model position in the Fallen Christian's life. Family members, children, followers, and others usually are not in the position to tear down these walls. Only when Saul finally accepted David as God's anointed, did David succeed in breaking down some of the walls that caused Saul to fall.

Step 3: Don't Try to Reason with Him at First

This isn't a Peter. This person has an excuse for everything (Proverbs 26:16). He will always have an excuse. In fact, reasoning with him may be taken as a personal insult. How dare you minimize his difficulties, his pain! How dare you imply that he is not a good Christian!

I recall a particular woman who acted like this. She had many difficulties, many problems. When I tried to reason with her, give her some advice from the Scriptures, and even check on her salvation, she became offended and indignant. I had to back off. She didn't want my reason—she only wanted me to accept hers.

In most cases, when a Christian who fits this fallen type comes for counsel, it is not to get advice. It is to get someone to agree with his or her justifications. You can't argue them into recognizing their error. For many like this, looking good is more important than being good.

Step 4: He Must Believe He Is Acting Foolishly

In 1 Samuel 26:21, we see Saul finally realizing that he hasn't just done wrong, he's been foolish. That's the key. Many people who are like Saul will recognize that they've sinned, but they believe they did the best thing under the extreme circumstances.

Saul no longer pursued after David when he finally realized how foolishly he'd acted. He realized that his decisions weren't just the best of a bad bargain; they were bad decisions all the way around. A person like Saul must come to see this. They must stop justifying their actions. He must realize that there is no excuse.

Until there is recognition of how foolish he has been, there will never be true repentance or remorse. As long as he is convinced he did the best he could, or that circumstances conspired against him, or that he had no other choice, he will continue to live in his fallen state. He'll be in internal misery because the Holy Spirit will be in conflict with his own spirit, but he'll not let on he has made a mistake.

His own actions, foolish as they look to others, must come to be viewed with these same eyes before he will demonstrate remorse and a desire to change. This task cannot be done by anyone. You won't be able to convince him he is acting foolishly. He must come to this realization on his own through other circumstances, loss, and failure—but more importantly through love.

This is what David did. He demonstrated over and over again that his love caused him to act in a completely different way than Saul acted. When Saul realized that David's actions of love were being blessed, he finally realized how foolish his own actions were. This is all you can do. Show him what loving actions are really like!

Step 5: Make Sure You Are in a Position to Help

King Saul listened to no one. He was, literally, king of the hill. No one had the right, power, or influence to tell Saul he was acting like a fool. Until, after many failed attempts to kill David, Saul finally realized that David was indeed the Lord's anointed.

In 1 Samuel 26:25, Saul tells David that he has finally come to realize that David would both do great things and prevail. I believe Saul, though reluctantly, finally understood that David was God's choice to succeed him to the throne of Israel. Having accepted that, Saul was finally able to look at his own actions through new eyes.

If David was really God's choice, then fighting David would be the same as fighting God. Thus, all of Saul's actions in the pursuit of David suddenly looked very foolish. This opening of the eyes is something that must happen to any Christian that is fallen as Saul was.

But to accomplish it, it may take a father, a boss, a Sunday School teacher, a pastor, a successful and influential friend, or a role model to get this Fallen Christian to open his eyes to his own foolishness.

As discussed, showing what actions of love really look like—how right Christian living should really be done—is what such a Christian must see. And he must respect the one doing it. Without that respect, he will simply refuse to acknowledge it.

If you are not the right person for the job, determine who that person might be. Enlist them and assist them in helping to try and bring this person back to the cause of Jesus Christ.

Step 6: Wait for a Shock or Scare Before Reasoning

David twice had the chance to kill Saul and didn't. Saul believed that David was out to usurp his throne and kill his sons. He believed it so wholeheartedly that he murdered the Lord's priests for helping David. Saul was clearly wrong, but he hounded David time after time after time, trying to kill him. David had to get Saul to realize he was wrong and the only way to do that was to shock Saul.

When Saul realized that God had delivered him up into David's hands, Saul recoiled emotionally and spiritually. God was willing to let David kill him—and David chose not to! The devastating shock that Saul felt was enough to shake him into humility!

For others, this shock could come in many different forms—a car accident, cancer, a ruined marriage, shattered health, financial disaster, losing a loved one, or even being overlooked. The shock usually has to be self-made. Saul created the situation with David, not the other way around.

In counseling, I have succeeded, on occasion, to shock someone into realizing the path he is taking is leading to disaster. Occasionally, a lazy husband will ask me to fix his wife. He is the greater problem, not her, but he refuses to see it that way. He is a Saul. In his eyes, his actions have been done because he has had no other choice. His behavior has been forced on him due to his wife's issues or problems. In order to change him, I have to shake him up from those beliefs. To do that, I sometimes take a half hour and just outline how every decision, every action, he has taken has just compounded, added, and created the problems in his marriage. Hopefully, having come from the pastor, he is shocked into sensibility. It has worked. On numerous occasions, a "Saul" has been shocked into realizing where the actual problems are and achieved the humility to do something about them.

But by and large, the shock must be of his own making. He has to be humbled by God. Your job is to love him and watch for that moment. When it comes, he will need someone, and you may be able to step in and help restore him to Christ.

Step 7: You Must Be Humble Around Him

This is the tricky part. Often the Christian who is in the best position to do this is the Christian who has been hurt by this Saul type. David humbled himself before Saul, proving that he had no intention of killing the king. Saul reeled from shock, realizing his enemy had done what he himself would not dare to do. This, more than anything, convinced Saul of the error of his ways.

Fallen Christians of this type need someone who will not look down their superior noses, or turn their arrogant backs, or shut them out. When they are hurt—shocked—they'll need someone to demonstrate love. This Fallen Christian will need to know that he can come back.

David did this by categorically stating he would not dare raise his hand against the Lord's anointed. He told Saul that his life was precious to David. This humbled Saul.

The person who has been hurt the most by such a Fallen Christian needs to deliver a message of love while the fallen one is still reeling from the shock of how foolish he has been. Then, and only then, will he come to his senses. Humility is easier to achieve when someone else has already demonstrated incredible humility. David's humility toward Saul was reciprocated.

The Saul type is more difficult to restore. They must first see the truth of their excuses and justifications. Reasoning with them will only exacerbate the problem. They need to be shocked into seeing it. You must hover around the fringe of the individual's life— close enough that when they hit that shock of their life, you'll be there to hold out a helping hand. Sometimes the shock can be delivered by an authority figure or role model. You may need to enlist help.

The shock will come (Isaiah 24:18a). These types retain the outward look of Christianity and so never stray very far from where they need to be physically. But there will come a time when God will prove the wisdom of the world to be merely foolishness (1 Corinthians 1:20). Be patient, pray, and love them.

A Word to This Type of Fallen Christian

Naturally, if you are such a Christian as described in this chapter, I hope that you will recognize that sin, even when done with such good intentions, has only led you astray and is causing damage to your spirit, the cause of Christ, and your church family.

I am not deluded enough, however, to think that you recognize yet that you are the person described in this chapter. You have all your excuses and justifications arrayed around you like a force field. You resist all attempts at reason, thinking others are unreasonable. But if that is you, then there is a simple little test I dare you to take. If you think you are not this type of Fallen Christian, then my little test should not be difficult to do.

I dare you.

First, pick three people in your life that you look up to and that you have access to. Schedule an appointment with each of them and ask them a series of three questions each. Ask them to be bluntly truthful in their answers. Here are the three questions:

1. What am I doing wrong that you think I am completely blind to?
2. Do you think I am doing anything that is directly or indirectly hurting the cause of Christ?

3. Is there anything that I have done or am doing that is hurting you or causing you emotional grief as my friend?

Did the answers surprise you? Do you dare to even ask them? If you are indeed the type of Christian described in this chapter, I only hope that the answers shocked you enough to realize how foolish some of your actions have been.

And if so, know this: welcome back! Humility is what every Christian must strive for and once you have found it, everything changes. You will find your relationships ten times stronger and your walk with God more vibrant than ever before.

Welcome back!

5

The Prodigal Son's Fall – Loved Pleasure

Text to Study: Luke 15:11–32

Characteristics and Signs of This Fallen Type

1. Believes the world can bring him happiness.
2. Is materialistic and selfish.
3. Resents authority.
4. Is often young—between 16 and 25.
5. Often can only be restored when he comes to his senses.

Why Did the Prodigal Son Fall?

At first glance, there seems to be no reason for the Prodigal Son to leave home. He has all the things that seem to be good to us. He had loving parents, a good job, money, position, and prestige. So why then did he embark on his riotous living?

There are two possible answers. First, he, like so many Christians, got caught up in what the world had to offer. Again, this is something that Jesus warned about in the Parable of the Sower:

> *Matthew 13:22 – He also that received seed among the thorns is he that heareth the word; and the care of this world, and the deceitfulness of riches, choke the word, and he becometh unfruitful.*

Riches, the party life, and the high-profile social life are all very attractive to people. They are instant gratifications that play to our core nature of self-preservation and therefore self-interest. This mentality often leads into things like gambling, alcohol, drugs, and sexual perversions. And it is an expensive lifestyle requiring lots of money to maintain. Soon enough, the Prodigal ran out of money, ran out of friends, and ran out of options.

People who indulge in the world often find themselves seeking any means to snatch as much instant gratification as possible. The long term has no bearing on their thinking; it is only what can be gotten now that matters. It's much like winning the lottery. For most, the winning of such large sums of money destroys them. The first thing they see is what the money can bring right now. It consumes them. The fortune required to win the lottery rarely brings the wisdom necessary to maintain the winnings. The Prodigal didn't earn his money, he inherited it. And he squandered it.

Obviously, this mentality is diametrically opposed to the Christian lifestyle. God is like cash up front, and the Devil is like a credit card. To enjoy the things of God, we often must pay the price first. We have to make the necessary sacrifices before we get to enjoy the benefits of God's blessings. But the worldly lifestyle is organized just the opposite. It is like a credit card. You get what you want right now and you can defer the cost later. And what does it matter if you can't afford to pay it? You merely need to make payments with interest—usually for the rest of your life.

The second reason for the Prodigal Son's fall may be his rejection of authority. He was the second son. He had an inheritance coming, but not like his older brother. He may have chafed under the weight of his father's authority. A wise father would seek to prepare his son for the difficulties in life he may face when he ventures out. Perhaps he hated the rules, the lessons, and being told what to do. He saw the city life as an escape from the tedious responsibilities and the pressure of always being in the background.

I've often found that the emotional feelings that come with authority issues can shift a person's thinking toward worldly living. The world presents itself as an escape from a responsible life to one of carefree and fun living. Many seek it, trying to rid themselves of responsibility and duty.

Many of the people who resent authority become angry, bitter, and spiteful. They seek to pacify these emotions by indulging in instant gratification. Many young Christians who grow up in loving Christian homes find themselves resenting the rules, the responsibilities, the duties, and the care of the Christian life. They want to be free from it.

This may have happened to the Prodigal Son. He fell through trying to free himself from authority, rules, and structure—or he simply became enamored of the sparkling life of a worldly lifestyle and got sucked in, his pride and lusts getting the better of him.

Outward Signs to Look For

More often than not, it is the young adult who grew up in a good home and even attended church who falls victim to the Prodigal Son syndrome. For the parents, pastors, youth pastors, and concerned friend, here are some of the typical signs to look for. If you see these signs, there is a good chance they are headed in the Prodigal Son's footsteps.

1. *Believes that instant gratification is the key to happiness.*

2. *Gets caught up in worldly possessions and lifestyles.*

3. *Often resents authority and refuses to listen to advice.*

4. *Tends to live riotously (or to excess, a type of rage).*

5. *Is very selfish.*

6. *Is often a young person—between the ages of 16 and 25.*

7. *May have grown up under a strict structure and resents the perceived lack of freedom.*

8. *Often has grown up in a good home and very possibly attended church since childhood.*

How to Restore This Type of Fallen Christian

To be frank, the Prodigal's father initiated a solution to restore his son that is quite troubling to me as a parent and pastor. I find his solution, which did work, difficult to accept and even more difficult to implement. Pay close attention to the following paragraphs. Despite the seemingly incongruent means, there is also much hope provided in the father's solution.

He let his son go.

He gave him the money and goods, and he let him go. As far as we know, he didn't argue with him. He didn't refuse his son's wish. He didn't fight him. He didn't even try to con him or trick him into staying. He just let him go. It is possible that the parable simply doesn't relate that part of the story, but what is obvious is that when someone gets to the point where they are going to walk away no matter what is said or done, you need to let them go.

The father exercised incredible wisdom here, despite what must have been an incredibly difficult thing to do. Let us examine the means by which he restored his son, one you may have to employ for your loved one or friend.

Step 1: You Need to Let Him Go (Luke 15:12)

People who choose the worldly lifestyle won't be interested in Christian things. They are mutually exclusive. Trying to offer a Christian lifestyle to someone interested in a worldly lifestyle won't work—especially if the person in question has yet to understand the consequences of the worldly lifestyle. They've made their choice. I recall a conversation with three older teenagers. I asked one of them if he wouldn't want to know how to go to Heaven. Here is how the conversation went:

"Wouldn't you want to know for sure that you're going to heaven?" I asked.

He looked at me funny and shrugged. "Nope. I want to take my chances."

"Chances? That doesn't make any sense," I insisted. "What if you were going to get on an airplane and I came to you and asked, 'Would you like to know if there is enough fuel on the plane to get you to your destination?' You'd be an idiot to say, 'Nope, I'll take my chances.' Wouldn't you?"

He shrugged again. "Probably."

"So wouldn't you like to know how to go to Heaven?"

"Nope."

About that time another teenager spoke up, "I'm kinda an atheist. I mean I know there's something—okay a God, I guess, but I read the Bible and I don't believe in most of that stuff."

"You read the Bible," I replied, hardly hiding my skepticism. "You've even read the book of Hezekiah?"

"Sure."

"There's no such book," I pointed out.

"Well, I don't believe all that stuff about not drinking, and not taking drugs, not cussing, and not smoking."

"So you're an atheist because you think God's an idiot? How old are you?"

"Sixteen," he replied, blundering into the trap.

"Ah," I muttered, deciding not to spring the obvious trap. I looked at all three of the boys and asked once again, "Are any of you interested in how to not go to Hell?"

They looked at each other and one after another said, "Nope."

I had to just let them go. There was no way to reason with them. I had better arguments, made more sense, but they didn't want to be told they couldn't indulge in their lifestyle. At this point the only thing anyone can do is pray for them. Give them over to God and hope that at some point in their future they realize their errors and come to their senses.

At the same time, fighting with them would only push them away further. Have you ever said something in a moment of pride and then later regretted it, but maintained the pretense because you didn't want to seem weak? If I attacked them, told them they were fools, idiots, and damned to Hell, I would erase any potential of helping them in the future when they do come to their senses.

Don't shut the door on someone like this. Don't say, "If you do this, then I never want to see you again!" or, "You are no son of mine. I disown you," or, "One of these days you'll find out I'm right and I'll laugh at you when you do," or, "Don't come crawling back here when things don't work out." Saying something like this robs you of any chance you have of getting them back one day. Don't slam the door shut. Let them walk out, but make sure they know it is open for them to come back.

The most important thing to do for someone like this is to pray for them. You may have to let them go, but that does not mean you have to let them loose from your prayer life. Pray and seek God on their behalf.

Step 2: Don't Bail Him Out (Luke 15:14–16)

You can't live the worldly lifestyle without having to eventually pay for it. The payment never equals the pleasures derived. There is always interest to pay (Luke 15:14–16).

The Prodigal Son ended up in the hog pen eating what the hogs refused to eat. Even so, this is not the time to run and bail him out of his misery. Not yet. I believe the Prodigal Son's father knew where his son was and the trouble he'd gotten himself into. But the father didn't bail him out. He didn't come to his rescue. To bail him out at this time would only encourage him to continue in the life he has so far led. He'll even begin to expect you to bail him out of future problems he creates.

I know a couple that has several adult children. At least one of the adult children never matured into the adult she should have been.

As a result, she lived her life much like the Prodigal Son did. She lived for instant gratification and self-serving. She has at least five kids of her own—all, I believe, from a different father. She preyed on her parent's sympathies and love, milking them for whatever she could get.

She took it and treated them like dirt at the same time. She began to feel entitled and, in my opinion, abused her parents. They'd pay her rent, buy her furniture, pay the car payments, and babysit the kids so she could go party regardless of her parents' schedules and needs. She'd get into disaster after disaster, and every time she needed to be bailed out, she'd harangue her parents into doing it.

On several occasions, I lovingly advised them to let her go. Let her get hurt and have no way out. That is difficult for parents to do, especially parents who feel guilty for not raising the kids right in the first place. In their case, the grandchildren would be the main focus of their reasoning to constantly bail out their daughter. It is a wonderful sentiment, but it never worked. She would constantly get into trouble.

She will never come to herself until the parents step away and let her pay the price for her own decisions. Only then can she see how stupid and terrible her decisions are. Only then can she possibly come to herself. Only then can the parents really help her like they want to.

Don't run to them when they get into trouble. Calling you up for help is not necessarily a sign that they are trying to come back. Bailing them out will only encourage them to continue in their destructive lifestyle.

Step 3: Wait for Him to Come to Himself (Luke 15:17)

There will come a point, usually at rock bottom, that he comes to himself. Only when he is willing to admit his error and choose to pay the consequences can you actually restore this kind of Fallen Christian. You don't have to chastise him. You don't have to berate him. You don't have to say, "I told you so." You just get excited that he's decided to come back.

I wonder how many of these Fallen Christians finally came to themselves but when they tried to come back, the "spiritual" Christians turned up their noses and turned their backs? How many have we lost because a wayward Christian had no place to come back to?

The question, however, is how to determine if someone has really come to his senses or is just trying to manipulate you even more. Here are some things to look for:

1. *He seeks you out.* Not to bail him out, but to just be accepted by you. He's not looking for succor, but is willing to endure even the minimum of your affection and love—if only you will take him back.

2. *Humility.* This is so important. If he has been humbled, seeks no one to blame other than himself, is willing to do whatever it takes to correct his mistake, and doesn't get angry at you or others for his own mistakes, then you can assume he is properly humbled.

3. *Admission of sin and guilt.* If he is willing to take responsibility, not blame bad luck, bad friends, or bad circumstances, but himself and himself alone, then it may be time to accept him back.

4. *A desire for a fresh start*—not where he left off—just a fresh start at the bottom.

5. *Willing to pay the price.* He doesn't want you to bail him out. He just wants to know that paying the price doesn't mean losing everything. Other than that, he will pay it.

I suspect that if you can find those five things, he's turned the corner. Bring him back with joy!

Step 4: Take Him Back with Joy (Luke 15:22–23)

Get excited that they came back. Brag on them for making such a wise and humbling decision. Don't dwell on the mistake. Don't be standoffish. Get excited. The Prodigal's father threw a party!

There is no one, and I mean no one, who won't react positively to joy and love. I have a cousin who years ago decided he didn't need God, religion, or church. At the time, he lived with my family. As a teenager, I argued with him, debated his reasoning, and even yelled at him a time or two, to no avail. He still wanted to do his own thing. My parents wisely let him go. His life became a mess.

Years later, I ended up talking to him on the phone. He didn't believe that I would ever accept him or even like him. He felt alone, isolated, and hated. But when I reacted with joy and love to talking with him, he responded positively. A direct result of which is that he went back to church for a time, until he slipped back into his old ways and started blaming everyone else again. I suspect there will come a time when he may come back.

Acceptance is a huge part of our makeup. Finding acceptance is one of the joys we long for. Give it to him.

Step 5: Defend Him from the Critics (Luke 15:31–32)

There will always be the critic who can't believe that you are so forgiving, so generous, so helpful to this Fallen Christian. Worse, they won't believe that the fallen one can come back and so may attack you and the fallen one. Defend him. Do as the father did when his eldest son criticized how his father reacted to the Prodigal Son's return.

Restoring fallen ones back to Christ is a command of God. It is a sacred duty. It is a wonderful way to serve God. Don't let anyone tear that service down. A Christian who returns to the fold will be very sensitive to criticism. He needs to know that there are people out there who believe in him.

__Hebrews 12:11–13__ — Now no chastening for the present seemeth to be joyous, but grievous: nevertheless afterward it

> *yieldeth the peaceable fruit of righteousness unto them which are exercised thereby. Wherefore lift up the hands which hang down, and the feeble knees; And make straight paths for your feet, lest that which is lame be turned out of the way; but let it rather be healed.*

After a Christian has been chastened, we need to strengthen him. Defend him from the sanctimonious critics. Eventually he will be integrated back into the Christian lifestyle and become a productive member.

A Word to This Type of Fallen Christian

If you fall into this category of Fallen Christians, I want to encourage you to take responsibility for the things that have gone wrong in your life. I understand that not all of it is your fault, but some, if not most, is a direct result of the decisions you made.

Only by deciding to take responsibility for your responsibilities will you get past this stage in your life. This is the essence of maturity. Maturity isn't about age or knowledge; it is about accepting and then taking responsibility. Once you do that, you will cease to be a victim and become someone with the power to make a real change in your life.

The Bible warns us about encouraging folly:

> ***Proverbs 26:4–5*** *– Answer not a fool according to his folly, lest thou also be like unto him. Answer a fool according to his folly, lest he be wise in his own conceit.*

The verses are a bit of a puzzle. The first one against warns what happens when we don't answer your folly. We end up participating in it, since you will most likely take our silence as agreement. The second verse tells us that we need to challenge your folly so that you don't think you are doing the right thing or continue to do it.

One of the best ways to do that is by letting you go and not bailing you out of all the troubles you get yourself into. Know this: we love you, but we also know that the only way you are going to come out of this with any ability to get ahead is for you to start taking responsibility for your responsibilities.

Don't be deceived by the sparkles and glitter of the world. Death and destruction always lurk in the shadows of lust and pride. You may have issues with authority, having a desire to live your life the way you want without restrictions. That only works in a world where there are no other people or a God to share it with.

No, life doesn't work that way. The strength of relationships all depend upon these rules—both spoken and unspoken. If anything goes, your relationships suffer. It is in these relationships that true joy and happiness in life are found—not a lifestyle of shameless greed and lust. The Prodigal Son lost everything because of his lifestyle, and no doubt your own relationships are suffering as well if you fit into this category of Fallen Christians—or soon will when the sparkle fades and the Devil is ready to call in your debts.

You could define maturity as the ability to set strong rules for your own relationships, rules you live by for the sake of the relationship. Do that, and you won't ever have a problem with the Bible or God telling you what to do—you'll already see the benefits of doing it!

We will let you grow up the hard way. Once you get it, there is always an open door and an open hand for you.

6

Judas Iscariot's Fall – Besetting Sin

Text to Study: Matthew 27:1–8

Characteristics and Signs of This Fallen Type

1. Is usually an addict or has a repetitive sin he either can't conquer or doesn't want to conquer.
2. Justifies his addiction by claiming or thinking no one suffers because of his addiction.
3. His choices are not born out of any logic or sense, just the need to fuel his addiction.
4. Doesn't think his addiction or sin is serious.
5. Doesn't realize how much harm he is bringing to the relationships around him.
6. Always has good intentions, even in evil acts.

Why Did Judas Betray Jesus Christ?

An argument could be made that Judas never did fall because he was never a Christian. This may be true in light of the fact that

Satan entered into him (Luke 22:3). But it is also true that Judas was chosen by Jesus Christ to be a disciple. In fact, Judas, for whatever reason, remained loyal to Jesus when others abandoned Him after being told the hardships of being a disciple (John 6:66–67). I think Judas had good intentions of being the right person. Jesus never had a lot of money, so even though Judas was a thief, Jesus was a lousy mark. There were much richer and wealthier targets to go after. So why tag along with Jesus?

We may never know this side of Heaven. But despite his greed and addiction to money, he may have had good intentions to change and saw Jesus as the avenue to change.

What needs to be addressed, however, is the fact that after seeing all that Jesus did, watching the miracles and observing the power of God, Judas still betrayed Jesus. Why? I think there are two basic factors that contributed to his betrayal.

First, Judas had a sin that he'd never taken care of—thievery or greed (John 12:6). This besetting sin constantly arose to consume Judas. It became an addiction, a need that had to be filled in order to bring even temporary satisfaction. Like any addiction, his decisions would be filtered through his desires.

Secondly, Judas probably believed that his betrayal of Christ would come to nothing as far as Jesus was concerned. It is very likely that Judas didn't believe Jesus would be condemned let alone crucified. Matthew 27:3 is where he realizes that his plan has failed. Jesus never sought to defend Himself and was condemned. Judas tried to put things right but could not.

Judas betrayed Christ believing that Jesus would do as He had done before when confronted with a mob bent on either killing Him or crowning Him. In the past, Jesus always escaped (Luke 4:28–30, John 10:39, John 8:59). No one could even lay a hand on Jesus. So when the opportunity presented itself for Judas to get richer without hurting anyone, his sin—his addiction—overrode his good sense. He betrayed Christ. He just hadn't figured that Jesus wouldn't try to escape or walk away as He had in the past. He hadn't counted on

Jesus refusing to even say a word in His own defense or pulling a miracle to free Himself.

Realizing what he had done and unable to come to terms with it, Judas committed suicide.

Outward Signs to Look For

What to look out for with this type of fallen Christian:

1. *He has an addiction or a besetting sin.* It may be secret or others may be aware of it, but it is constantly there and he often returns to it again and again (Proverbs 26:11).

2. *He will often look good in every other area of his life.* He may be a faithful church member, a Sunday School teacher, a bus worker, an usher, or a dynamite soul winner.

3. *His resistance to his besetting sin is thin.* Opportunity to indulge in it will often be an overwhelming desire. He will do so at the expense of others—even those he cares about. Often this is spontaneous or merely a short-term plan.

4. *He will justify his sin by thinking that if no one gets hurt it can't be that bad.* He may convince himself that it is only temporary, or a one-time thing.

5. *He is more apt to allow Satan to deceive him.* His addiction or besetting sin makes him vulnerable to the prompting and oppression of the Devil. His skewed thinking and judgment begin to manifest in odd ways—as Judas did when questioning why the ointment for Jesus' feet hadn't been sold for money (John 12:5–6). His reasoning will be just a bit off, just a bit skewed because of the sin in his life.

6. *He WILL hurt someone he cares about eventually.* This is unavoidable. Any addiction will channel decisions through intense desires. These overriding desires will cause him to hurt someone he cares about. In most cases, it is unintentional, but it happens nonetheless.

7. *He will often show remorse and regret for the pain his sin has brought others.* He will often make an effort to fix or correct what he has done.

8. *He can become suicidal if he feels his mistake is beyond redemption.* Addictions that lead to pain and suffering are hard to deal with. The guilt is nearly equally as powerful as the desire. The two tear at each other like two strange alley cats thrust into a small room together. The resulting depression has caused many to feel suicidal.

How to Restore This Type of Fallen Christian

I believe that Judas could've been redeemed. If someone had reached him at the right moment, he might have given his life to Christ, not committed suicide, and possibly become a powerhouse for the cause of Jesus. Who knows, God could've even used him to write a book of the Bible.

But because there was no Restorer for Judas, we never learn what he might have become. Instead, we read of a tragedy. Here are a few thoughts and ideas on what you might do to restore this type of Fallen Christian:

Step 1: Pray for Him

Prayer, to open the eyes of such a Fallen Christian, is essential. The Restorer who does not pray will not be equipped to help. Who prayed for Judas? Jesus did, I am sure, but what about the other disciples? Did any of them pray for the man? We have no record of it.

Pray.

Step 2: Miracles, Proof, and Reason Are Not Persuasive

Judas had all the proof he wanted of Jesus' divinity and of His being the Messiah. He may even have believed in these things, but he couldn't bring himself to trust Jesus. Maybe he did what a lot of other people do and just put it off "until I get straightened out first!" For three years, Judas walked with the Saviour and still betrayed Him. So just being in a good church, surrounded by good people, and carrying the right Bible is not enough sometimes to bring the addict around.

Our tendency to return to our own folly is an aspect of the curse of sin our bodies are enslaved to. These people don't deny Christ. They are often saved, attend church, and serve Christ in some aspect. They don't need to be convinced. They are already.

The problem is their actions, motives, and decisions are funneled through their addictions. It skews things until a decision or action is taken that hurts someone else. Have you ever tried to reason with an alcoholic? In most cases he will agree with you, nod his head, and return to his drink.

Step 3: Hurting Someone He Loves Is Persuasive

Experience has taught me that until this type of Fallen Christian has hurt someone he loves or loses someone he loves as a direct result of his addiction, it will be difficult to restore him. His addiction is, in his own mind, merely a minor hiccup in his life—nothing that he must fixate on or really worry about. Only after his plans crash and burn and others burn with him will he finally truly regret his addiction or besetting sin.

People who seek help for addictions are usually those with marriages falling apart, estranged children, huge financial burdens, or destroyed health, and those who have lost the affection and respect of friends and peers. Think about it—if you could keep everything important to you and keep your addiction, would you give it up? Probably not.

The best time to help such a Fallen Christian is when they are at this weakened state of life. Here is where a Restorer can step in. Here is where a Restorer can repair a life and bring a Fallen Christian back to the fold.

Step 4: Restore Him When He Tries to Fix His Mistake

Therein is the heart of the issue. If he comes to you to fix his mistake, that usually means you were the one who crashed and burned in his sin as well. You might be his wife or her husband, a child, or a friend. The odds are he hurt you. If you reject him as the elders did Judas, you may push him away forever. This is your one big opportunity to reclaim a Christian for the cause of Christ. You need to swallow your pain, your heartache, your anger, and your fears. You need to help him.

You may not want to, but you need to. Too many people allow their own pain and anger to dominate their reaction to someone trying to come back. It is not for you to say if they deserve a second chance. It is not for you to determine who should be restored and who should not!

It takes a mature individual who is willing to swallow his own pain and help the very person who brought the pain to begin with.

You may believe that he deserves no second chance. Perhaps, but Judas never helped anyone or shared Jesus with anyone the moment he killed himself. If he had been restored, he might very well have made a positive difference in someone's life. And for that someone, it would have been all the difference in the world!

Step 5: Allow Him the Chance to Fix His Mistake

Judas never got the opportunity to correct his mistake. He tried and did everything he could, but he wasn't allowed to. If you don't allow someone the opportunity to fix his error, he may never come back. If you were the one that got hurt, it may take a lot for you to give him a second chance. But you must give it. You must give him the opportunity to try to fix his mistake.

Trust plays a huge factor here. Having been hurt by him, you will no longer trust him. This will give rise to suspicion and the construction of emotional walls to protect you from allowing him to hurt you again. You cannot allow your fear of future pain to rob you of future blessings.

I recall a particular wife who discovered her husband's affair. She was understandably bitter, angry, and in tremendous pain. She wanted with all her heart to make the marriage work. He, remorseful of his indiscretion, also wanted to make it work. Yet she feared every effort required to make it work. She didn't want to get hurt again. She resisted much of my advice because of that fear. Her fear was preventing the very thing she so desperately wanted—a wonderful husband and marriage. It took a while, but eventually she focused on her hope in Christ, not her fear of being hurt.

This is essential to any Restorer. Don't allow your fear of pain to rob you of the hope of a wonderful relationship.

Step 6: Make the Second Chance an Admonition

In other words, make an aspect of the second chance an action against his addiction or besetting sin. If he is an alcoholic, make him pour out all the booze in front of witnesses. Force him to seek counsel for his problem. Make him accountable for his time and money spent. Praise him for every success—small or great. Whatever his besetting sin is, force him to move against it.

I once told a drug addict that he needed to turn in every supplier he knew. That scared him for he feared retribution. He didn't do it, and so he still struggles with it to this day because, I believe, he never took action against his addiction. He just tried to bury it in a corner, but addictions never lie still.

Imagine if Paul had never taken action against his former position of killing and imprisoning Christians. Paul's change of heart led him to attack his previous beliefs, stance, and popularity. In so doing, he shut the door from ever going back. He made going back to his old life difficult. In fact, the one time he did try to make it look like he'd gone back, it backfired on him. No one would believe it.

I like the story of how some of the conquistadors burned their ships after making landfall in America. They made it very difficult to go back. We need to make it difficult to go back to our sin.

There is a difference between a sinful bad habit and a sinful addiction. A bad habit can be conquered easily enough, but an addiction needs to be constantly attacked. Not just guarded against—attacked. Billy Sunday became the foremost preacher against alcoholism in his day. Frequently, entire towns would dry up after one of his revivals against booze and moonshine. But then Billy Sunday had once been an alcoholic himself. His attack on his former addiction allowed healing, brought him peace, and gave him a wonderful marriage and ministry.

Jesus is the key to any deliverance, however. The best attack against the gates of hell is by launching sorties at it from the church, bombarding it with artillery of the Scriptures, ramming it with the battering-ram of the blood of Jesus, and lifting high the standard of the cross on the field of battle.

The business of the church is to win souls. It is also to destroy any hellish stronghold that would seek to protect a perversion, a sin, or a wicked addiction in someone's life. When helping someone to overcome an addiction, direct them to attack it—wage war against it and plant the standard of Jesus Christ in the midst of that battlefield.

2 Corinthians 10:3–6 – For though we walk in the flesh, we do not war after the flesh: (For the weapons of our warfare are not carnal, but mighty through God to the pulling down of strong holds;) Casting down imaginations, and every high thing that exalteth itself against the knowledge of God, and bringing into captivity every thought to the obedience of Christ; 6 And having in a readiness to revenge all disobedience, when your obedience is fulfilled.

Every addict needs to do what the above verse teaches. But they need something more. They need a Restorer.

2 Timothy 2:24–26 – And the servant of the Lord must not strive; but be gentle unto all men, apt to teach, patient, In meekness instructing those that oppose themselves; if God

> *peradventure will give them repentance to the acknowledging
> of the truth; And that they may recover themselves out of the
> snare of the devil, who are taken captive by him at his will.*

The Fallen Christian needs someone who will help him come to the truth and then recover himself from the snare of the Devil.

A Word to This Type of Fallen Christian

A bit of warning for you: an addiction is never a problem until it hurts someone you love. Once you hurt someone you love, you will have to try and gather up the pieces—a very, very painful prospect. The problem is that you don't think it ever will be a problem—not for you, anyway.

This type of thinking is incredibly dangerous. The fact that you must justify it with such a statement is proof itself. A loving relationship is one where sacrifices are made for the sake of the relationship. No relationship can exist on selfishness alone, and ultimately your addiction is the height of selfishness.

You will put the addiction before your marriage, your children, your friends, those you respect, and your parents. You may not think that it will hurt anyone, but you are wrong. The very fact that you are willing to put the addiction first is indicative of damaged relationships.

Don't let your addiction control your thinking. Get help. Few will actually follow this advice because, again, you don't think there is really a problem.

But when you hurt someone you love—and you will—there are several things I want you to remember and do.

First, don't let the rejection of your efforts to fix your mistake cause you to give up. That is what Judas did. He couldn't fix the mistake, so he quit—quit on life. Don't you do that. People are going to find it hard to trust you. Accept that as a normal consequence of your action and determine you are going to win their trust back! Determine you will do what it takes to earn it.

Secondly, be proactive against your addiction. People are going to want to see if you are really going to change. Too many addicts claim they are reformed but go right back to it. Attack your addiction as strongly as you once sought to fulfill it.

Thirdly, make God the center of your life. Be careful here. Don't swap your addiction for service. Service to God is fine and wonderful, but it can never take the place of a real relationship with God. Focus on the relationship with God and the rest will fall into place.

Fourthly, there are Christians who love you. You do not have to fight this battle alone. If you feel you are, then you are either pushing people away or you need to go meet some new Christians. Either way, allow us to help you.

7

King David's Fall – Sin of Passion

Text to Study: 2 Samuel 11:1–27

Characteristics and Signs of This Fallen Type

1. Falls due to a fit of passion.
2. Lets his guard down and was in the wrong place, at wrong time, with wrong friends, or had wrong influences.
3. Does his best to hide his sin or failure.
4. May continue to sin in an effort to cover up previous sins.
5. Typical behavior changes, often out of character.
6. Unlikely to be restored until caught.

Why Did King David Fall?

Even the best of Christians can fall. And I mean that literally. There is no such thing as an exempt individual, and David is certainly an example of how the mighty can fall. He was a man after God's own heart, to be sure, but he committed adultery with a woman and then conspired to have her husband assassinated to cover his sin. But why? Why did he do this?

To begin with, he wasn't where he should have been (2 Samuel 11:1). His reasons or excuses for not being where he should have been—fighting a war against the enemies of God's people—may be complicated or simple. He may have stayed home due to simple exhaustion or being war weary. Perhaps he just wanted a break. How many Christians can relate to being burned out, tired, or weary in service? We often fall so easily into sin when we are tired. Perhaps David felt overconfident in his army's abilities and didn't think he was needed.

No matter what the reasons were, however, I don't think he was planning on sinning. I don't believe he stayed behind with the express purpose of committing adultery and murder.

I believe he let his guard down. This, more than not being where he was supposed to be, is probably why he fell. Satan can learn of our weaknesses, our faults, our fleshly appetites, and when one is discovered, he will leverage that weakness against us the moment our guard is let down. The difficulties and pressures of life often wear on us like sandpaper. If we are not careful, we find ourselves worn down to a spiritual nub, having failed to renew our spirit in the Lord. Satan or our own fleshly appetites will then take over and breach our lowered guard. The result? We sin.

The Scriptures warn us not to give place to the Devil (Ephesians 4:27). We can't afford to give him any maneuvering room to attack us. Nor can we give our flesh any opportunity either, as one often leads to the other. Yet David did. He allowed his guard to be lowered and he saw a beautiful woman bathing on a roof top. Did he know she would be there? Doubtful. His reaction was clearly, to me anyway, spontaneous and reactionary. His fleshly appetites rose up to steal his moral convictions. He fell into adultery and, soon after, murder.

This was a sin of passion that just got out of control. All passion sins have this tendency. It's not premeditated. It's not thought out. It's not even well planned out. It just happens when our guard is down and suddenly we are taken unawares, overwhelmed by lust. This is something every Christian can relate to. We're all guilty of doing this. We all get caught up in the moment, and we allow our fleshly desires to take over. We jump out of the spirit and into the flesh in a moment of weakness, passion, and lust.

This can only be avoided by a conscious effort to remain in Christ Jesus. When we slip out of that effort, we become vulnerable to our fleshly appetites.

Knowing he had done wrong, David perpetuated another sin to cover up the first one. This is common enough. How often do we tell a second lie to cover for the first one? He continued in this manner until exposed.

David's fall is typical of many fallen giants of the faith. A fit of passion and a ministry is destroyed, a bright future burned out, or a role model turned into a negative preaching example. The Davids of the world need to be restored. They need a Restorer.

Outward Signs to Look For

This type of fallen Christian is fairly easy to spot if you know what to look for. Sins of passion are rarely masked well.

1. *He will try to hide it, even if that means sinning further (2 Samuel 12:12).* He won't try to justify it, he will just try to cover it over. This marks the distinction between a Saul type and a David Type. Saul would seek to justify it. Saul wanted to convince everyone that his wrong was in fact right. David never believed what he did was right in any way. He just sought to hide it.

2. *He will publicly condemn his own sin (without naming himself as the culprit), believe it a sin, preach that it is a sin, and even fight against this type of sin (2 Samuel 12:5–6).* David condemned the villain in Nathan's contrived little story, not realizing Nathan had him pegged as the villain. In fact, David got enraged over the story Nathan told. Many people preach against a sin they have in their own lives. It is interesting

how some people who struggle with a particular sin will often be the most vocal against it.

3. *His behavior will become erratic and strange—desperate perhaps.* David went out of his way to try and get Uriah drunk, hoping he would go home, lie with his wife, and assume the child born afterwards was his own. Failing that, David resorted to outright assassination. The lengths David went to hide his sin were him out of character. Look for these odd actions that are just out of character for the person in question. You may discover they are trying to hide a sin.

4. *This person will regret his sin.* He will feel badly about it once his sin is brought out into the open. Exposed, he will show remorse. He may wear his guilt on his sleeve, becoming overly sensitive to any hint of exposure, but once exposed, his embarrassment over the sin will cause him to face it. But while he is trying to hide it, his behavior turns erratic and odd. This is often a sign of guilt.

This is the kind of Christian we most often identify as a hypocrite. Truthfully, we are all hypocrites in some manner and in some way. A hypocrite isn't irredeemable. He has both the understanding and knowledge that what he is doing is wrong. However, he will try to pretend he doesn't have a problem. Until he is willing to see the sin in his own life, he won't be redeemable.

How to Restore This Type of Fallen Christian

This type of fallen Christian is fairly easy to restore. Sins of passion are very common among Christians, unfortunately, and are among the easiest to restore, fortunately. Often, once their sin is exposed, they turn into the Peter type already discussed. Here are a few pointers for the Restorer:

Step 1: Pray for Him

This may seem like a broken record. But there is no way to underestimate the power of prayer.

As a young teenager, I am ashamed to admit, I had a lying problem. I often would lie for no particular reason, other than lying had become a habit for me. Once, I compounded that sin with another—theft. I stole $20.00 from my younger brother and lied about where I had gotten it. My mother knew I was lying, but my story of where I had gotten the money was plausible. There was no way to prove or disprove my lie. She came up with a novel approach to the problem.

She prayed for me.

In fact, she went to the church altar after a Sunday service and prayed for me. Her prayer, as she relates it, went something like this, "Father, I know my son is lying. Would you do whatever you have to do, to get him to admit it?" Giving God carte-blanche to do whatever He wants to do to your son takes a bit of bravery—or is the result of a very, very exasperated mother. God answered her prayer.

I was sitting in the pew still, quite proud of how well my lie and theft had gone off. Suddenly, an emotional weight fell on me unlike any I had ever before experienced. Emotions raged in my heart and mind and a pressure built on me where I felt I was being squeezed from every possible angle. Only one thing rose to the surface of that turmoil—my theft and lie. My teenage mind had never experienced this before. I suddenly feared God was going to kill me right then and there!

I jumped up from my seat and literally ran down the aisle to find my mother. I met her coming back. I grabbed her and nearly wailed out, "Mom! I did it! I took the money from my brother!"

She regarded me without emotion or expression. "I know," she replied simply. She brushed by me to return to the pew. I was left in the aisle devastated and with only one option. To get it right. So I did. Thank God for the prayers of a mother.

Thank God for the prayers of a Restorer.

Step 2: This Person Needs to be Caught

Once he is caught, he will no longer try to hide his sin. Hiding it from others is also his way of hiding it from himself. He won't deal with the sin until he no longer can hide it. In fact, once exposed, it is a relief to have the sin out in the open. For many people in this situation, having it out in the open relieves them of the burden of it, allows them to focus on getting it right instead of hiding it. Amazingly, many of these types of Fallen Christians will suddenly become calm, rational, and willing to correct their errors! Before being caught, they acted erratically, were overly sensitive to what other people said or did and added other sins to hide the first one.

In some cases after the exposure, they resort to the Peter type described in chapter 2. They get embarrassed about their sin, feel like a failure, and may feel others are condemning them. Read the chapter on the Peter type for more information on how to restore a person like this, if one you are trying to help seems to turn in this direction. Look at his reaction to being caught. In many cases, if you are appropriately loving and forgiving, he will come back with little effort.

He needs to know that his sin is no longer hidden, as Nathan exposed David's sin. Hiding it further would just be a waste of time. Once this is accepted, restoration can take place.

Step 3: Don't Embarrass Him Publicly

As far as I can tell, Nathan the prophet went to David alone. He didn't denounce him in front of David's family and friends. He merely let David know that God and he both knew of his sin.

If you discover that someone has committed a sin of passion, you need to let them know that you are aware of it and offer help. Again, for most people, having someone else aware of their sin comes as a great relief—an embarrassing one to be sure, but a relief nonetheless. He is now free to deal with it appropriately.

But be careful of making a spectacle of the sin. The Bible clearly tells us that we are first to go to a fellow believer privately to fix problems (Matthew 18:15). Embarrassing a Fallen Christian will only push them away and make it difficult to help them come back. With that in mind, don't ever gossip. A talebearer, the Scriptures teach, hurts more than anything else. In fact, we are not to meddle with such a person (Proverbs 20:19).

Step 4: Make Sure You Are in the Position to Help

It took someone in authority to shake the admission out of David. Joab, who served David, could do nothing to change David's mind. David even forced his general to be complicit in his sin. Nathan, however, represented the Lord Himself. That relationship gave the prophet enough clout to confront David and help him.

It may be that you need to have earned the Fallen Christian's respect before you are in the position to confront him about his sin. If he doesn't honor or respect you, he may fight you on it. In some cases, you may recruit someone you know he respects to help you. This is not gossip as long as you are actively trying to recruit real help. Telling someone who can do nothing, however, is gossip.

For example, occasionally I become aware of a sin of a member of a different church. I won't confront this person because I am not in a position to help. However, if I know both the Fallen Christian and the other pastor, I will call his pastor up and explain the situation and recruit his help to be a Restorer. Telling my own church members, however, would accomplish nothing and therefore be nothing but destructive gossip.

Step 5: Don't Minimize the Consequences

This type of Fallen Christian is willing to pay the price. He knows he needs to. He knows there are consequences. Let him pay them. Show mercy later if need be, but don't minimize the consequences.

Suffering the consequences accomplishes several things. First, it will serve as a constant reminder not to return to his sin. Second, it helps to purge the guilt that he labors under. This person doesn't hate God. This person loves God. Like David, he may even be a man after God's own heart. He needs the guilt purged. Suffering consequences helps to purge that guilt. I did wrong. I was punished. It's over. It's done. It's behind me. I can now move forward for Christ. That's how you want him to think.

You must have the Restorer's attitude to accomplish this. And you really need to be in the right position to restore this person. A child who witnessed an adult's sin will have difficulty restoring the adult because the child hasn't earned the respect and honor of that adult. The child will be shut down by the adult if he even attempts it.

There are always consequences to sin. If you remove those consequences, you remove one of the key motivations to do right. But consequences cannot be administered by someone who lacks the authority to do so. Can you imagine a child disciplining his parent? Doesn't work, does it? However, a pastor, a Sunday School teacher, a youth pastor, a parent, a teacher, a boss, a mentor, or government officials all have the capacity to administer consequences.

I recall a young couple that had a falling out with each other and some physical violence took place. The police were called. He ended up in jail overnight. Problems ensued. One of the consequences of his actions resulted in his being sentenced to domestic violence classes twice a week at $25.00 a class. That added up to $400.00 a month. Fairly expensive, wouldn't you say? He asked me to help him get out of the classes—he'd be taking them for about a year—but I refused. He argued that the classes weren't Christian, and that they didn't teach biblical principles. I agreed with him— they didn't. The success of those classes lay not in the teaching, but in the price that must be paid. Who wants to spend nearly $5,000 dollars and nearly 200 hours of your life just for the brief pleasure of hitting someone? Those programs rarely actually help someone change, but they do make people more restrained because they don't want to pay the price. They don't want to pay it again. It makes for a good deterrent.

I often ache when parents bail their kids out of trouble over and over again. They take away the deterrent, and their children grow up to be spoiled brats. Mercy is best used after the lesson has sunk home. It is better to tell a disobedient child that they are grounded for four weeks, and then after two weeks, when you are sure they got the lesson, you grant them mercy and remove the last weeks. This will actually endear them to you.

In the end, don't minimize the consequences of sin. Love them back. Help them. Suffer with them if necessary, but don't ever minimize the consequences of sin. The process of purging his guilt allows for restoration. Don't rob him of that.

A Word to This Type of Fallen Christian

If what is described in this chapter is you, then I beg you: don't continue to hide your sin anymore. Tell someone you respect and who you think will be willing to partner with you and help make amends.

Be willing to pay the price, the consequences of your actions. One of the main reasons we hide our sins is to avoid the consequences. Everyone does it. It always amuses me to hear of one Christian attacking another Christian because he attempted to hide a sin. I wonder what the first Christian is hiding.

Nevertheless, you are going to be stuck in spiritual quicksand until you deal with the sin in your life. I know you love God. No one is debating that. I know that once revealed, people are not going to trust you, and others will avoid you. I apologize for the hurt that you will suffer in this regard. But a whole lot more people will respect you if you just come out and deal with it. It is always worse when you are caught.

Recently, as of this writing, a mentor of mine was caught in and convicted of a crime and sentenced to years in prison. He held the respect and admiration of thousands, and in one moment of passion, he lost it all. He was a David of our time in many different ways. But now, I doubt there can be a more lonely individual on the planet. His enemies are rejoicing. His friends are confused and afraid—distancing themselves from both him and the crime. His family is hurting. And now this man, who once raised the banner high for the cause of Christ, is in jail. Understand, this individual was responsible for winning hundreds of thousands to Christ. He salvaged thousands of marriages. He set thousands of young people on a good path. He helped thousands out financially. He helped me. There are going to be many people in Heaven because of this man—more so, I dare say, than because of many law-abiding Christians. Few, however, will remember that. Most will only know him for his crime.

This is not in any way an endorsement of his crime. I believe he should go to jail. I believe he should pay for his crime. But it is for these reasons that you are trying to hide your sin. You don't want to go through what this man is going through. You don't want to pay the price.

But remember, no matter what happens to him, he is not beyond the grace and mercy of our loving Saviour. God still loves him. God still wants to use him. God hasn't abandoned him. How dare we hate someone God loves? I don't, and there are many others who don't either.

And God still loves you. Even if everyone else attacks you and turns on you, it is better than dying internally, dying spiritually because you have set yourself against God and stand at a distance to Him. A sin that is not dealt with is worse than everything my mentor is suffering, because it will poison everything else you do. Everything you touch will be shaded in the color of your sin—in your own eyes. This is worse. My friend who committed the crime can now work on moving forward. That, at least, is a much better situation.

Proverbs 24:16 *– For a just man falleth seven times, and riseth up again: but the wicked shall fall into mischief.*

You may have noticed something interesting about this verse. In God's eyes, the man who fell wasn't just because he never fell, but because when he did fall, he got right back up again. That's the key. Get back up!

I pray that you come to realize this truth in your own life. Stop trying to hide it. Quit living a hypocritical life. Get it right. Make it right. Then you can put it behind you. Then you can move on.

For His sake!

8

King Solomon's Fall – Wrong Influences

Text to Study: 1 Kings 11:1–10

Characteristics and Signs of This Fallen Type

1. Is usually surrounded by bad influences.
2. Often runs with the wrong crowd.
3. Allows his opinions to be swayed by those he fears to be in conflict with.
4. Actions will often be about appeasing those he runs with.
5. Will tend to ignore his own wisdom and knowledge in order to make a certain person or group happy.

Why Did King Solomon Fall?

According to Scriptures, Solomon was the wisest man who has ever lived (1 Kings 3:12, 4:29–32). Yet he made such a tragic and, from our vantage point, stupid error that it is hard for many to believe that he can even be in the running for such a title. His heart was turned from God by the influence of others. How could such a wise man make such a mistake?

The key to Solomon's fall is found in one verse:

> ***1 Kings 11:4*** *– For it came to pass, when Solomon was old, that his wives turned away his heart after other gods: and his heart was not perfect with the LORD his God, as was the heart of David his father.*

Solomon fell victim to one of history's classic blunders: he chose the wrong people to love. 1 King 11:1 tells us that Solomon loved many strange women—a direct violation of God's command found in Exodus 34:16. Solomon had seven hundred wives and three hundred concubines. This is an amazing number—a thousand women! If he just spent a single day with each of them in a rotation, it would take nearly three years just to get to each of them.

Many of these marriages were political arrangements, cementing peace treaties, tribute amounts, and borders. This was a common practice, and apparently, Solomon indulged in the custom with great enthusiasm.

Still, that doesn't explain how Solomon could make such a mistake given all the wisdom God had granted to him. Doesn't wisdom preclude making mistakes? Don't we label people who make good decisions as wise and those that don't as unwise? Since Solomon made such a massive mistake, how can we claim he was the wisest man who ever lived outside of Jesus Christ?

In truth, all of us have been known to allow our desires to override our good sense. So many Christians that fall do so with eyes wide open. They know it to be a mistake before they do it. But why then do it? When we allow a fleshly appetite to dominate our minds, it trumps any and all wisdom we may possess.

There are many definitions of wisdom. But the most direct is this: knowing when, where, how, and why to use the knowledge you possess. However, knowing when to apply knowledge does not automatically mean you will do so. Even knowing you are making a mistake does not stop you from making it.

> *1 Kings 11:1–2 – But king Solomon loved many strange women, together with the daughter of Pharaoh, women of the Moabites, Ammonites, Edomites, Zidonians, and Hittites; Of the nations concerning which the LORD said unto the children of Israel, Ye shall not go in to them, neither shall they come in unto you: for surely they will turn away your heart after their gods: Solomon clave unto these in love.*

The word "love," used twice in these verses, is not the deep, abiding love that we normally attribute to a husband and wife. This word means affection, generally in a sexual sense. Solomon had a massive sexual appetite that he found to be insatiable. But this in itself did not cause him to fall.

His appetite allowed the reason for his fall to happen, but it was not the cause of his fall directly. No, the real reason Solomon fell was because he allowed all these women into his life and they changed his heart.

> *1 Kings 11:3 – And he had seven hundred wives, princesses, and three hundred concubines: and his wives turned away his heart.*

When Solomon's pursuit of his appetite allowed all these influences to come into his life, they changed his heart. These women who worshipped false gods, who hailed from a different culture, ran with a different crowd, and were involved with unholy practices changed Solomon's heart—this despite his full awareness of the danger. Notice what he wrote to his own son:

> *Proverbs 5:3–6 – For the lips of a strange woman drop as an honeycomb, and her mouth is smoother than oil: But her end is bitter as wormwood, sharp as a twoedged sword.*

> *Her feet go down to death; her steps take hold on hell. Lest thou shouldest ponder the path of life, her ways are moveable, that thou canst not know them.*

He knew the dangers intimately. He had enough wisdom to recognize them and even warn his son. Yet he still fell prey to a trap he could clearly see. Why? That I can't say. I can speculate. Perhaps he wanted to avoid conflict with his wives—many of them princesses of powerful neighbors. Perhaps he became weary of trying to do right in the face of so much wrong. Perhaps he feared the loss of indulging in his appetite if he didn't give in to his wives' demands.

And regardless of how you look at it, these women became important to him. His love translated into a need, and it poisoned his heart. Those who have been in Christian circles for a time have most likely witnessed a godly young man or woman get mixed up in the wrong crowd. Regardless of the reason, all their good sense is tossed out the window when they begin the process of trying to fit in and belong.

So many young people have been led astray by this one thing: the wrong influences.

Outward Signs to Look For

1. *It is usually a desire, lust, or need that pulls him away from the Christian influence and toward these other influences that cause him to stumble.* In the search for fulfillment, a Christian will look toward those he supposes will fulfill it. This is where this Christian can best be restored. If it gets to the next sign in this list, restoration becomes much more difficult.

2. *His choice of friends will change.* One of the more obvious signs is when a Christian changes the crowd he runs with. People are important, and who you make important is who you allow to influence you. This type of Fallen Christian will often change his friends.

3. *His attitude changes as a result of the change of friends.* Because these new friends become important to him (a type of love), his perspectives, opinions, likes, and dislikes also change. A once happy Christian turns into a bitter, resentful Christian.

4. *Eventually, the outside comes to reflect the inside.* Many Fallen Christians successfully hide their change of heart or mind, living a hypocritical life. After a time, they just give up even the pretense of a Christian life. Solomon began building idols and sanctifying ground to false gods.

5. *Bitterness becomes the staple of his thinking.* When you read Ecclesiastes, you see a bitter old man—a far cry from the Song of Solomon—who had everything he could ever want, except a joyful heart. His wisdom allowed him to recognize the dangers, realize his own failings, understand his own end, and regret his decisions. Not a fun way to live.

6. *He will betray those who he once loved.* Having switched friends, he cannot continue to love both (Matthew 6:24). He will invariably hurt those he once claimed to love.

How to Restore This Type of Fallen Christian

Step 1: Pray for Him

Prayer is important, but it is important in many ways that we don't suspect. A Fallen Christian of the type described here will have hurt those who have loved and invested in his life. Often the one who is hurt is the Restorer or someone the Restorer loves as well. This makes it difficult to approach such a Fallen Christian in the right spirit.

This is where prayer comes in. Prayer will change your own attitudes toward the person you are seeking to restore. Prayer will remind you that God still loves this Fallen Christian and so should you.

But loving such a person can be problematic when you have been hurt. Prayer gives you the right focus and perspective as well as an outlet to actually love him.

Pray.

Step 2: Isolate Him from His Influences

There is absolutely nothing you can do when he is surrounded by those new influences in his life. Unless you can isolate him from his chosen influences, you have no hope of influencing him to return.

I can't advise you on how to do this. Sometimes it is as simple as catching him at a vulnerable moment when his other friends are not around or have left, being uncomfortable with his problems. Perhaps you can invite him out to eat or over to your house. Each individual is different, and many will resist your efforts.

This doesn't change the fact that your influence won't be as potent if he is surrounded by others whose opinions he values more. This is the major difficulty with this type of Fallen Christian. Solomon spent his life surrounded by these women, and they dominated the influences in his life. Things would no doubt have gone different if he had simply married a godly woman and stuck with her.

You can't force isolation from the wrong influences without resistance. You need to wait for the right moment where you can step in and make a difference.

Step 3: Have Compassion on Him

The Bible teaches:

***Jude 1:22–23** – And of some have compassion, making a difference: And others save with fear, pulling them out of the fire; hating even the garment spotted by the flesh.*

The first part of the verse is what we will deal with here. The last part will be dealt with in the next point. Jesus showed compassion and made a difference in the lives of many people (Matthew 14:14, 15:32, and 20:34). This sort of Fallen Christian will not be cajoled, argued back, or yanked back forcibly. What he needs is someone to have compassion on his plight.

Solomon was so rich, so powerful, so far above the common man that I seriously doubt anyone had much compassion for his plight. From all outward perspectives, he had it all. He had everything—except joy. We don't know, but maybe if someone had had compassion for him and tried to make a real difference, things would have turned out differently. But who would be in a position that Solomon would actually listen to him?

Again, however, this difference needs to be made away from the tainted power of the Fallen Christian's worldly friends and influences, lest the taint spoil your efforts.

When dealing with a teenager who has gotten himself caught up in the wrong crowd, I follow these principles used by Jesus on Peter, after Peter had quit the ministry and went back to his old life and influences:

1. *I never attack his wrong friends or challenge his decisions in who he chose as a friend*—it is already too late, and he will resent having his choices challenged. (Jesus never challenged Peter's decision to go fishing in John 21.)

2. *I help him in ways that his friends could or would never do.* I look for ways to make a difference in his life that are beyond what his friends or other influences could do or would do. (Jesus not only had a fish cooking for the empty-handed fishermen, he also told them where they could catch a great quantity of fish.)

3. *Once the difference has been made, I ask him if his friends would have been able to make such a difference or if they would have hindered it.* This gets him to thinking. (Jesus began contrasting Peter's fishing to his service to God. He asked Peter if he really loved Him more than the fish.)

4. *I then redefine his concept of friendship.* I explain what a true friend does or would do. I show him what a true friend would do. This also gets him thinking. (Jesus redefined for Peter the entire notion of serving Jesus and what the qualifications were.)

Does it always work? No. It depends largely on how isolated he is from these other influences at the time. Many Fallen Christians of this type, particularly young ones, don't want to risk losing these other relationships. It is your job to make him want a friendship with you more.

These principles are the ones that Jesus used over and over again in dealing with people around Him. So often, Jesus changed someone's opinion by simply redefining the concept (Mark 3:31–35).

Step 4: Save with Fear, Pulling Them Out (Jude 23)

Most Christians read that verse from Jude and assume that we need to terrorize someone into coming back to Christ or even into getting saved. This has led to things being said and done that aren't in line with how Christ teaches us to treat people. The word "fear" means to be terrorized. However, I am not convinced that the verse is suggesting that we terrorize another Christian—or even an unbeliever—in order to save him.

The example is of pulling him from the fire lest he be burned or killed. Imagine such a situation. Imagine someone you love falling into the fire. Who is terrorized? I submit that both of you are terrorized. The verse tells us to save some with fear—not by fear. The preposition I would expect here, if the verse is indeed implying that we need to terrorize someone into salvation, would be "by." Instead, "with" is used.

When you see that someone you love is walking into danger, it should terrorize you. If it does not, then perhaps you don't love him as you claim. For me, it terrifies me to see my children caught up in drugs, alcohol, or some other sinful lifestyle. This fear, if you will, causes me to act. It causes me to pull them out of the fire.

Here then is the key to the verse. I believe the teaching here is that sometimes compassion is not enough. Sometimes you have to be truly scared for someone—scared enough to act, to pull him out of the fire he is walking into.

A Fallen Christian needs to know there are people who are scared enough to go to extraordinary lengths on his behalf. If he sees you laboring for hours in prayer, if he sees your tears, your fear, your concern, if he sees your desperation and worry for him—if he sees these things, then maybe it will shake some sensibility back into him.

This Fallen Christian needs to know that he matters to someone in Christian circles. He needs to know that his actions are causing someone else to fear.

A Word to This Type of Fallen Christian

If you are this type of Fallen Christian, then you probably have already dismissed this writing or justified your choice of influences in your life. But I do have a prayer for you. I pray that you realize how detrimental your new friends are to your life. I pray that you realize how many people you are terrorizing as they watch you spiral away from everything you once loved.

Friends matter. I know. And no doubt you believe your friends matter to you. It is for this reason that you so desperately cling to them, willing to throw away all the values of Christianity your pastor, parents, and old friends tried to teach you.

Perhaps you see freedom—like the prodigal son did—in these new friends and new loves. Perhaps you have fallen in love and you are now willing to compromise your values and morals just to keep that person near. Let me say this: If you must lower your values or morals to keep a friend near, then you have not gained a friend. You've gained a slave's chain to be manipulated and used. You are not a better person for it.

I beg you, choose your friends carefully. Your heart is not so fixed that it cannot be changed. Indeed, your opinions and values are often associated with the crowd you run with.

Proverbs 4:23 – *Keep thy heart with all diligence; for out of it are the issues of life.*

— 83 —

9

Cain's Fall – Angry at Being Slighted

Text to Study: Genesis 4:1–15

Characteristics and Signs of This Fallen Type

1. Is usually a very angry person because someone let him down or betrayed him.
2. Feels cheated and slighted—perhaps even by God.
3. If his anger is not held in check, he may cross a line that cannot be ignored.
4. Struggles with controlling his anger.

Why Did Cain Fall?

In a word: anger. Cain felt cheated and slighted by God. He didn't understand why God rejected his offering and yet accepted Abel's. He may have felt that Able had somehow made him look bad, and the notion of it seethed until he erupted in rage toward his brother.

Resentment built up in his heart and he finally just exploded. His anger consumed him to the point where he finally rose up and killed his brother. We don't know if Cain premeditated the murder or if it was a murder of passion and rage. I tend to hold to the latter, myself, but in either case, anger fueled his actions.

Anger causes all of us to do things we would not do under other circumstances. The Bible tells us to be angry and sin not (Ephesians 4:26). This implies that anger itself is not a sin, but most generally leads to a sin. So anger itself may not be wrong, but selfish anger always leads to selfish actions.

Once a sin of anger is committed—not matter the reasons—you are now dealing with a Fallen Christian.

Outward Signs to Look For

Most people already are very familiar with this type of Fallen Christian. Angry people show anger. It's easy to spot. But here are some specifics to look for:

1. *He expresses anger—usually with his mouth.* But his body language will also be telling. He will not look happy. He will look sad, or angry, or resentful, or grumpy. We use the term "carry a chip on his shoulder" to describe this person. He may throw a pity party in an effort to be noticed or attract attention. He may be vengeful and seek allies to support him in his vengeance.

2. *His anger will begin to dominate his thinking even over the positives in his life.* Selfish anger has the tendency to override and destroy even the good things that come to a person's life. How many people have left a church because of their anger over something the preacher or a fellow Christian said? It doesn't matter that for the last ten years they've agreed with practically everything else, or that they have enjoyed wonderful fellowship, blessings, love, and help for all of those years. This one thing—this tiny little thing—settles

in their heart and burns in their mind, overriding everything else.

3. *He will refuse to see himself as the reason for his problems.* He will blame someone else. He will focus on someone else as the source of his unhappiness, rejection, or failure. He may respond in a pseudo-politically correct way by agreeing that some of the problem may be his fault, but he will not budge from his anger or resentment.

4. *He will most likely have violent outbursts.* Anger can only build up to a point before you snap. Cain did. He killed his brother. These violent outbursts may be suppressed in public but come out in private, over the phone, at home, with a buddy, in a counseling session, or in a chance meeting. As the Restorer, counselor, or pastor, you may never witness these outbursts, but the odds are you will hear of them from those closest to the Fallen Christian.

5. *He will use his emotions as leverage.* Because of his frustration and anger, he will use them as an excuse for whatever action he intends to take. He will claim he needs to leave the church because of how bad it is, although only he can really see how bad it is. He will make ultimatums to get his way—a very "him or me" approach.

For this type of Fallen Christian, the danger lies in crossing a line that cannot be ignored. When something is done out of anger that goes too far, they add embarrassment, guilt, and fear to their anger. Suddenly, you can add fear of fellow Christians to the symptoms listed above. When this happens, they believe that they have ruined everything and blown any chance of fixing the problem. In an effort to protect their own emotions, they may even begin treating Christianity and the people of Christ as enemies. Be watchful of this.

How to Restore This Type of Fallen Christian

As far as we know, Cain was never restored. On the contrary, he was banished for the rest of his life. He fled from God, feared for his very existence, and nursed his anger and resentment in exile. He spawned a whole generation of children and grandchildren that abandoned God and indulged in evil and wickedness.

But Cain's failure to be restored wasn't due to a lack of effort. God tried to reach out to Cain, but Cain would have none of it. His anger wouldn't allow him to see clearly enough to realize that he was the source of his greatest problem.

Remember, you can only restore someone who wishes to be restored. And there is another problem as I've already mentioned. Anger can cause you to step over a line of seemingly no return. Cain killed a man. He crossed a line—a line that God couldn't ignore. The best chance of restoring this Christian is before their anger causes them to cross a line like Cain did.

Here are some thoughts on that:

Step 1: Pray for Him

If prayer is our access to God, then why in the world do we not begin every endeavor with prayer? The Bible warns us that the Restorer must be humble and meek, and there is no better way to achieve that than by laboring in prayer.

Fasting helps too, particularly when you pray and fast. Life is made of relationships, and the strength of your relationships will determine the earthly joy you have in this life. If this is the case, laboring in prayer is one of the greatest gifts you can give to any relationship.

Step 2: Go to Him When You First Notice Anger

God went to Cain as soon as Cain's countenance fell. He tried to reach out to Cain right away. The longer someone sits on resentment, the stronger it grows. Try to get to him before this happens. So many couples come to me for marital counseling when their resentment for each other has reached epic proportions. It's incredibly difficult to help people who have allowed their anger to consume them.

Proverbs 15:1 – A soft answer turneth away wrath: but grievous words stir up anger.

Proverbs 15:18 – A wrathful man stirreth up strife: but he that is slow to anger appeaseth strife.

Once anger becomes a way of life for a person, he will barricade away his heart and begin to look at everyone and everything with suspicion. Anger, selfish anger, is truly a danger to the Fallen Christian—particularly if the Fallen Christian believes he has been dealt with unjustly. Even sincere offers of good intentions will be twisted around to fit into fueling his anger.

I recall asking a fellow to help me heal the heartache of a fallen brother in Christ. I failed to realize that the first person resented the fallen brother because he thought I liked the fallen brother more than I liked him. It wasn't true, but his resentment twisted my offer to team up into a demeaning action against him. If I had noticed the signs of anger sooner, I may have been able to prevent a serious problem.

Look for the signs of anger and resentment. Sometimes they manifest themselves in envy and jealousy. If you see it, you may need to become a Restorer. Try to head it off before it becomes something serious. Once it is serious, it is hard to heal.

Step 3: Get Him to Open Up to You

Cain, as far as we can tell, never discussed his resentment and anger toward God and his brother with anyone. God inquired about it, trying to get him to open up, but Cain resisted. Perhaps if he hadn't resisted, he may have found solace. But he was too angry to discuss it, and he was too angry to listen either. When he did discuss it with his brother later, his anger consumed him, and he rose up and killed Abel.

It is essential to get a person to open up to you about his anger. Imagine the anger being like infection in a wound. In order for the wound to heal, you need to get the infection out. The anger cannot be permitted to abide in his heart. You need to draw it out, lance the wound, and clean it thoroughly.

If you can't get him to open up to you, you may need to find someone with whom he can. The Restorer isn't God, nor is he granted unusual spiritual powers. The Restorer is usually someone who cares. If you can't help, find someone who can.

Step 4: Try to Give Another Perspective on the Problem

God tried to get Cain to understand some basic things that he had misunderstood, but Cain was simply too angry to listen. Still, there is truth and a lesson to be learned from God's attempt to restore Cain. A person will hold onto his anger for as long as he believes the anger is justified.

Proverbs 14:9 teaches us that a person who is slow to wrath is of great understanding. In other words, your anger or lack of it is largely dependent on your ability to see things from completely different perspectives. Greater understanding often helps you to control your anger.

In the past, I've been very successful at moderating someone's anger by giving him two or three different ways of looking at the circumstances that made him so upset. It is interesting to watch as his anger seeps away when he realizes there might be more to it than he originally supposed.

For example, someone cuts you off while driving. Your instinct is to get upset at the other person's reckless driving. Your actions often reflect this in what you say, your own reactionary driving, your use of the horn, or the gestures you deliver in retaliation. You might rethink your anger if your passenger said, "I saw a pregnant woman in the car with him. He might be taking her to the hospital!" Instead of getting angry, you may whisper a prayer for their safe journey.

Another example may drive this home more fully. Pretend you come home to find someone had broken into your house and raided your kitchen. You find spilled cans, broken bottles, knocked over boxes, and the refrigerator door left open. Your natural reaction is to get angry at the violation and the intrusion into your domain. But if I hauled a scrawny, eleven-year-old girl up to your door and informed you I'd caught the thief, and you discovered that the poor girl hadn't eaten anything for a week and a half and that she was practically starved crazy, you may not get so angry. You may decide to give the thief some food!

Again, so much of our anger is dependent on our own selfish perspective. Here is how our actions are formulated:

1.   Behavior is dependent on our attitude.
2.   Attitude is dependent on our perspective.
3.   Perspective is formed by the influences and circumstances we have been exposed to.

To actively change someone's behavior, it is necessary to expose them to another way of thinking—another perspective.

Step 5: If You Are Involved, Apologize

If the Fallen Christian's anger is directed at you, you may need to apologize even if you don't think you did anything wrong. No matter how true that may be, you can still apologize for hurting them. You can still apologize for the way it came across or for your inability to convey it correctly to them so they could understand.

Don't make an issue of it or try to defend yourself. Any effort you make to defend yourself will only fuel his anger. To disarm him, you simply apologize and make some effort to try to make up for it. The Restorer has to be the more spiritual of the two and he has to be willing to bear the other person's burdens, even if it hurts or is unjustified.

I remember a church member who became greatly offended at something I said about the lack of wisdom in buying a new car because, by so doing, you incur a debt you cannot pay off by selling the car. What I didn't know was that the church member had just purchased a brand-new car the day before and assumed I was talking about him. He assumed I was on some vendetta about his purchase, when actually I had no idea about the car or his feelings for weeks. He didn't come to church for a time, and I grew concerned so I went to see him. Imagine my surprise at learning that a simple statement about debt could be taken so out of context! What did I do? I apologized. I did everything I could to defuse his anger.

You need to feel that a Fallen Christian's restoration is more important than your own pride and feelings of justification. "Only by pride cometh contention," Proverbs 13:10 teaches us. Drop your pride. Apologize if you can.

Step 6: Warn Them of the Dangers of Their Anger

God told Cain that sin was near. He tried to warn Cain that he was standing on the brink of a dangerous precipice, one from which he might never be able to fully recover, if he fell off. For Cain, his anger became all-consuming; he ignored the warning.

But that doesn't mean you shouldn't warn other fallen believers. You may have to, with love, paint a picture for them of what might happen if they continue down the road of anger.

As a pastor, I have a plethora of illustrations that I use to warn people of what might happen if they continue down the path of anger. Anger, we know, is not a sin in itself. But when anger is selfish, it never works the righteousness of God. Never. I've seen marriages crumble because of anger and resentment. I've seen people die because of it. I've seen people jailed because of it. I've seen people lose loved ones because of it. I've seen futures destroyed, hopes crumble, dreams poisoned, and bodies deteriorate because of anger.

A woman who attended our church for a short time had built up so much anger and resentment toward something a neighbor had done to her that she literally made herself sick. I told her she needed to let it go, that it was killing her. But she looked me right in the eye and said, "I'll never let it go. I don't care what it does to me."

Maybe if I could have reached her years before, when it all started, we could have helped her over it. But she had crossed a line. She held to her anger religiously, and it poisoned her own body.

If you can reach a person before that happens, you may be able to warn him off. I recall a young lady who became greatly upset at what another woman in the church had said about her. I pulled her into my office once I discovered her anger and warned her about it. I explained where it could take her. I used her life as an example and painted a bleak picture of what her anger could do to her. It worked. This new perspective allowed her to let go, to heal.

A Word to This Type of Fallen Christian

If you are this type of Fallen Christian, you are no doubt looking for a way in your mind to hold on to your anger. I understand that you feel hurt, abused, or cheated—and perhaps even rightly so. But if you don't let your anger go, it will poison your heart and all of your relationships.

I challenge you to realize that relationships should be more important to you than holding on to your anger. I'm not talking about how the other person sees his relationship with you. I'm talking about you.

Joy in life will come from these God-given relationships. You need to think that your wife or husband, your friends, your children, your parents, your siblings, your brothers and sisters in Christ are more important than your anger.

Even if you get your revenge, your justice, what have you actually gained? You've damaged the relationship in exchange for a temporary emotion of satisfaction. What you lost is of eternal value.

Trust me—it is just not worth the trouble. Let go of your anger, find some help, surround yourself with people you love and cherish, and move on in your service for Christ.

10

Jonah's Fall – Authority Issues

Text to Study: Jonah 1:1–17

Characteristics and Signs of This Fallen Type

1. Doesn't like the way God says something is to be done.
2. Has authority issues in general.
3. Thinks he has a better way of serving God than God's way.
4. Is incredibly stubborn about doing things his way.
5. Is hard to reason with because he thinks he has already figured out what is best.
6. Thinks his actions are right even when doing wrong.

Why Did Jonah Fall?

Jonah disagreed with God's plan (Jonah 4:2) to spare Nineveh. Jonah wasn't the type of Christian who fell into sin. He didn't do anything that we would consider to be terribly wrong. He didn't start to drink, or cheat on his wife, or commit murder, or anything else we typically consider to be an act of sinful backsliding. Jonah simply disagreed with what God intended to do.

He had authority issues.

He thought he could force God's hand in order to change God's plan. This is always a mistake. Many Christians try the same thing—not only with God, but also with other authorities in their lives. We don't like the situation God has allowed to come into our lives, and we try to force God to change it. We pray and pray, or we become rebellious to the situation, or we fight against what God wants us to do.

Many Christians fall when they perceive the authority in their life to be wrong and they begin a campaign against it.

For Jonah, what he wanted overrode, in his mind, what God wanted. I believe Jonah was actually trying to be a martyr. I think he knew God typically used the most dominant military power to chastise Israel when she was backslidden. Nineveh was the capital of the Assyrian Empire. And Israel was indeed backslidden. I think Jonah feared that if Nineveh was spared, God would use the military arm of the Assyrians to punish Israel for her backslidden state.

Jonah was right.

God did eventually use Assyria and Nineveh to conquer the northern country of Israel (2 Kings 15:29). Anticipating this, Jonah wanted them all dead. He even argued with God about it (Jonah 4:2). If God destroyed Nineveh, then the Assyrian Empire would crumble and there would be no one to invade and punish Israel.

I think Jonah was trying to play the hero. If he forced God to kill him, then there would be no one to go and preach to Nineveh. This is evidenced by his lackadaisical attitude toward every effort God made to turn him around. He slept through the storm at sea while everyone else feared for their lives (Jonah 1:5). He told the sailors that they needed to throw him overboard to stop the storm, but he didn't bother jumping in to save their lives (Jonah 1:12–15). And exactly how long would you wait to begin praying to God if you were swallowed by a whale? Not three days and nights like Jonah did (Jonah 1:17, 2:1)!

When Jonah actually did get to the city, he didn't try to be convincing, but merely hastened through it and then sat down, hoping to see God destroy it (Jonah 3:4). In fact, he was willing to wait 40 days just to see God kill everyone. When that didn't happen, he got angry at God (Jonah 4:1).

Jonah fell because he didn't like God's plan. He didn't like where it would take him, where it would eventually lead, and what he would have to do.

Outward Signs to Look For

Here are some things to watch out for in this type of Fallen Christian. This Christian will become miserable in the will of God because he hasn't yielded to it. Indeed, he will begin seeing most authority through these same eyes. He'll begin to resent church, the pastor, or any other authority in his life.

1. *Knowing the will of God, he will intentionally run from it (Jonah 1:3).* He doesn't like it or even agree with it. He'll be willing to live in peaceful misery—an oxymoronic state—to escape the misery he believes lies in doing the will of God.

2. *He will most likely have authority issues in general.* If he is willing to defy God, he will be willing to defy his parents, law enforcement, his pastor, and his boss.

3. *He will truly believe his way is better and will be at peace with it* (Jonah could sleep peacefully in the midst of a dangerous storm, Jonah 1:5–6). I've met people who honestly thought God was wrong, and they had a better way. Many people try to do good their own way, and believe it is the better way. They are willing to even suffer for it. They are okay with God's punishment.

4. *He knows that God may come after him.* Many times, I've said to someone, "You understand that God won't be happy with what you do, don't you?" The person would smile almost patronizingly and reply, "God knows what is in my heart. He'll forgive me." This is such a dangerous attitude (Jonah 1:12). I can point out the Scriptural principle prohibiting his particular actions, and he won't be

bothered. He will believe this is something he has to do and God is welcome to punish him for it. He is a martyr for a sinful cause!

5. *He will be exceedingly stubborn.* Jonah took three days in a whale's belly before he couldn't take it anymore. And someone who has fallen like Jonah has also will be extremely stubborn and resistant to change (Jonah 1:17 and 2:1). He will resent advice. He will continue down a path of destruction despite all warnings to stop—even to facing a storm and a whale's belly.

6. *He will be very displeased with God's choices (Jonah 4:1) or the choices of other authorities in his life.* Watch out for someone who argues doctrine or methods based on their own understanding and logic and not biblical principles. For example, have you ever heard someone say, "Will God condemn me for putting my family first?" It becomes an excuse to explain why he can't obey the commands in the Bible. He will search for loopholes and even dredge up Scripture that looks to contradict the plain teachings of the Bible. I met a guy who went to extraordinary lengths to prove that God didn't condemn sex before marriage in any capacity—even to the point where he delved into the Greek and Hebrew to prove his point. His argument made sense only to him.

How to Restore This Type of Fallen Christian

This type of Christian is exceedingly difficult to bring back. Here is someone who is knowledgeable of the will of God but disagrees with it or doesn't like it. He refuses to acknowledge the authority in his life to give him direction. There are several things, however, the Restorer can do:

Step 1: Pray for Him

Keep this person before God. You want God's attention on this person, because the calling of God needs to be a hook and a draw back to the correct path. So pray for him!

Step 2: Be a Voice of Reason

God tried to reason with Jonah at the last. This is important. Jonah, as far as we can tell, didn't buy into it, but then the story ends. We don't know if Jonah ever accepted God's will as supreme. I don't know if God was really trying to convince Jonah or give him reasons to accept God's will at a later date.

Either way, be a voice of calm reason. God used a gourd to point out Jonah's flaw in his logic. God took the time! So must you. Don't expect agreement. Just give him something to think about.

If there are other people who agree, even in principle, with the authority the Fallen Christian disagrees with, then it may cause her to re-evaluate her thinking. For example, as a pastor, I would often have to challenge a teenager's rejection of her parents' authority. I would point out entire flaws in her logic, explain God's perspective, and show her how she could make a difference by changing her attitude and actions.

Some have agreed. Others just don't want anyone, no matter who it is, to reject their perceptions of, or desires regarding, how to do something. This doesn't mean you shouldn't explain it to them. This doesn't mean that they shouldn't know there are other people who back up the authority in their lives.

Step 3: Allow God's Calling to Attempt to Draw Him Back

Often, the only way to restore this type of Fallen Christian is for the person to experience the barbed grappling of God's calling.

Romans 11:29 *– For the gifts and calling of God are without repentance.*

God isn't just going to let this person go easily. In fact, if he runs from the will of God, he runs the risk that God will do extraordinary things to get him back on track. But once a person does come back, someone needs to be there to give him perspective. This is the key. This Fallen Christian will most likely have gone through unusual events in his defiance of the authority in his life. It will leave a mark on him spiritually, emotionally, mentally, and even physically.

Again, God used a gourd to make Jonah see that his selfish pity for the dead gourd—something that he had nothing to do with—is miniscule in comparison to God's pity on a people whom He had created.

It may take another Christian giving this fallen Christian the right perspective to bring him back all the way. This may only happen after God brings him back through His calling—or an authority's attempt to reign him in. All of our disagreements with God are a result of faulty logic, ignorance, lack of understanding, or warped perspective. God's ways are far above our ways.

> **Isaiah 55:8** – *For my thoughts are not your thoughts, neither are your ways my ways, saith the LORD.*

Disagreements with other authority may be different. The authority may actually be wrong. But mishandling that disagreement and the inability to yield to the decisions of those in charge creates a breech in the spirit. This rebellious attitude seeps over into the spiritual realm and damages his relationship with God.

The Restorer, in this case, must be patient and willing to have long talks with the Fallen Christian to help him understand that faith and trust in God's Word is more important than understanding something that might always be beyond his ability to fully grasp. Indeed, the challenge to trust in authority he perceives as wrong is a huge step in maturity.

You'll need to be experienced and have a solid footing in the Scriptures to do this. A young man in our church believed he had a better way of following God than what the Scriptures explained. He took a single verse out of context and created an entire doctrine around it. He wouldn't listen to reason at first, bucking the advice of older and wiser Christians. Only after he fell, and fell hard, was he willing to get the proper perspective on his sin nature.

A Word to This Type of Fallen Christian

May I submit to you that yielding to the authority in your life is more important than always being right. Obviously, if your authority is advocating a sin, you should resist, but to fight the authority in your life simply because you disagree with how they are doing things or with one thing that they said is not biblical.

> ***Romans 13:1–2*** *– Let every soul be subject unto the higher powers. For there is no power but of God: the powers that be are ordained of God. 2 Whosoever therefore resisteth the power, resisteth the ordinance of God: and they that resist shall receive to themselves damnation.*

The Bible is clear that resisting the authority in your life puts you in opposition to God. Resisting the leading of the Holy Spirit puts you at odds even with yourself. A Christian can't resist the Holy Spirit without negative consequences. Even bucking authority because you think you have a better way of doing something or because you just don't like the way it is being done will create a rebellious spirit that corrupts your spirit.

No one is going to agree with another person one hundred per cent of the time. It just won't happen. So unless you are being asked to do something contrary to the Word of God, you should submit to the authority in your life.

> ***Romans 13:5–7*** *– Wherefore ye must needs be subject, not only for wrath, but also for conscience sake. For this cause pay ye tribute also: for they are God's ministers, attending continually upon this very thing. Render therefore to all their*

> *dues: tribute to whom tribute is due; custom to whom custom;*
> *fear to whom fear; honour to whom honour.*

God explains in the Scriptures that submission to authority accomplishes two things. First, you do not incur the wrath of God. That in itself is a good reason to submit. Second, your own conscience will suffer if you don't. Rebellion is as the sin of witchcraft (1 Samuel 15:12). This rebellious spirit will eat away at you, corrupting your thinking, destroying your joy.

If you have authority issues, go to your authority and get it right—before it consumes you.

11

Absalom's Fall – Injustice and Revenge

Text to Study: 2 Samuel 13:19–34, 14:32–15:6

Characteristics and Signs of This Fallen Type

1. Becomes withdrawn and reclusive.
2. Believes that a great wrong has been committed against him—and is often correct.
3. May take it upon himself to fix the problem in an inappropriate manner.
4. Often plots to acquire his version of justice.
5. Will seek revenge.

Why Did Absalom Fall?

Hatred ruled Absalom's thinking (2 Samuel 13:22). He felt robbed of justice. Absalom's problem began when he found out that his older half-brother, Amnon, had raped his full sister, Tamar. Such an act would enrage any brother who cared. But to add insult to injury, their father, King David, did nothing about it. As far as I can tell, David gave Amnon a free pass on his sin.

According to the law, Amnon should have died for his sin (Deuteronomy 22:25–26). But Amnon was the heir to the throne of David. He was the oldest, and their father, King David, only displayed a small amount of anger at his eldest boy's rape of Tamar. After two years of waiting for his father to do something, Absalom decided to take matters into his own hands.

But during that two-year period, Absalom's anger and bitterness only grew. Finally, he planned and executed Amnon's murder. This was not a sin of passion like Cain committed; this was a cold blooded, pre-meditated, well-planned murder. To him, his actions weren't those of a backslider, but those of an avenger—a righter of wrongs. Very likely Absalom believed that his actions were merely those the king should have ordered anyway. He may have been right—it just wasn't his place to do it.

Absalom's fall did not come as a result of a sinful habit, a crime of passion, or someone's hurting him directly. No, his belief in the system was broken. He expected his father to react according to the law. But when his father did not, Absalom believed that the system and his father had failed him. He took matters into his own hands. This is why he fell. When he began to conspire against his brother, he allowed his rage, anger, and sense of injustice to rule his heart. He fell because he no longer had faith in the system to give his sister justice.

Outward Signs to Look For

1. *He becomes withdrawn and reclusive (2 Samuel 13:22).* If you see someone withdrawing from social gatherings or becoming quiet and fading into the background, this could be a sign he is harboring resentment in his heart. He may have a physical presence, but heart and mind are elsewhere.

2. *He believes that a great wrong has been committed and is angered that nothing or very little was done about it.* He will exhibit feelings

of betrayal and injustice. This injustice will become a pet peeve with him. He will see this injustice in every aspect of his life, often pointing it out to those around him.

3. *He believes the system has failed him.* It could be a church, a school, the government, or even Christianity as a whole. It could be an individual in authority. Regardless, he doesn't think justice has been done.

4. *He won't give straight answers to direct questions that have nothing to do with his grievance.* He may become ambivalent in his responses or attitudes toward people—particularly toward the person or system he feels did the wrong.

5. *He could suddenly do something exceedingly hurtful and devastating.* This would be in an effort to right the wrong or exact revenge—the same thing in his mind. This isn't the rage of Cain or the foolishness of Samson, but rather the cold, calculated, and premeditated action of someone in the bonds of hatred.

6. *He will feel betrayed when others don't cheer on his actions of justice or revenge.*

I would like to add that the qualities of this Fallen Christian are often manifested outside of Christian circles. To point out the more extreme cases of such bitterness and resentment, someone will take a gun and rampage through schools, political meetings, or former places of employment, killing and maiming people. These people feel like the system is so broken that the injustice done to them or others cannot be fixed. They will plan, as was done in 1999 at Columbine High School, to exact their own version of justice.

The typical person, Christian or otherwise, will rarely push things to such extremes. But I have dealt with teenage girls who purposely go out and have sex just to defy a drunken and abusive mother. I have dealt with wives who will cheat on their husbands because the husband did it first. I have dealt with former employees who will post slander on the Internet against ex-employers in an attempt to exact vengeance for an injustice that no one will do anything about.

In Christianity, this type of Fallen Christian can be very dangerous. Although there have been incidents of extreme violence committed by Fallen Christians as Absalom did, mostly they like to spread malicious rumors or plan a campaign of slander. It will be planned. It will be thought out.

Be careful not to fall into this type of person's crosshairs.

How to Restore This Type of Fallen Christian

For this type of Fallen Christian, there are two phases that needs to be addressed:

1. The vengeance phase
2. The post-vengeance phase

While the injustice, in the eyes of this Christian, remains, he will continue to seek his version of justice. Whatever he has planned will consume him and, unfortunately, the vengeance phase makes it much harder to restore this Fallen Christian.

Interestingly enough, after he has committed whatever sin he uses to enact his vengeance, he is much easier to restore. His vengeance will wound him spiritually and emotionally. A Restorer who can help such a person heal and seek forgiveness stands a fairly good chance of restoring him back to Christ.

Restoring This Fallen Christian in the Vengeance Phase

Step 1a: Pray for Him

In his case, prayer is essential. During this phase, he will build up a hedge of lies that he surrounds himself with. Understand that the initial wrong may, in fact, be absolutely true. For this type of Fallen Christian, he may not be making the injustice up. But to justify his own actions in trying to bring justice to the wrong, he will lie. He will even come to believe his own lies. Prayer will help in breaking down this hedge of lies.

Step 2a: Isolate His Perceived Injustice

The Restorer needs to know exactly what the Fallen Christian believes to be the injustice. You may discover that you actually agree with him. You may find yourself on the Fallen Christian's side. But even if that is the case, preventing him from acting out in vengeance is by far the better result than even achieving justice. His sense of vengeance, if allowed to take form, will leave him miserable and broken.

In either event, it is important to isolate what the injustice is. Without knowing what has caused the pain, anger, and hatred, you will not be in any position to help. Don't simply pass his problem off. Don't make light of it. Don't belittle it. Don't excuse it.

It is amazing how much pain and anger can be released if someone would just listen to his grievance. I have successfully restored many Christians just by listening to them as they describe the injustice. Just knowing someone else cares and is interested goes a long way toward restoring someone to the fellowship of Christ.

Step 3a: Determine If the Injustice Can Be Fixed or Not

There may be a simple solution to the problem. Once you have isolated the injustice, examine it for a solution. Often the solution is as simple as seeking clarification from the other side. So many of the injustices of the world are the direct result of a misunderstanding. That's it—a misunderstanding.

If you can fix the injustice, then the problem is solved. You can move on and so will the Fallen Christian. He can shift gears to a more productive Christian endeavor.

In some cases, the injustice can't be fixed. This may be due to the fact that the injustice is only imagined, or the other person involved is no longer around, or the other person involved has no desire, intention, or inclination to fix the problem. If so, you will need to tackle the problem from a different angle.

Step 4a: Explain True Vengeance and Forgiveness

Most people do not understand biblical vengeance, nor do they understand biblical forgiveness. If you can teach it correctly, explain it right, you may turn a person's course from doing something mighty stupid.

> ***Romans 12:19*** *– Dearly beloved, avenge not yourselves, but rather give place unto wrath: for it is written, Vengeance is mine; I will repay, saith the Lord.*

The only thing that vengeance accomplishes is producing a cycle of vengeance. Once it starts, it is incredibly difficult to break. Feuds are started this way. Great-great grandfather once hit so and so's great-great grandfather, and so generations later, members of each family still hate each other even though no one really knows why.

Here is what I might say to a person in this situation:

"You're set on doing this?" I may ask someone who's out for revenge.

"I am."

"So, you must hate your children then."

He looks at me strangely. "What are you talking about?"

"If you do what you intend to do—get even—you will drag your children into your petty squabble. How do you think the other guy's son will feel when you do what you intend to do to his father? You think he will like you for that? Do you think he will like your children for that? If he wants to get revenge on you for what you do, he just may take it out on your kids. So I ask you again, do you hate your children?"

"Well, I, well, my son can take it!"

"I see. You want him to grow up hating. You want him to act like you and to seek vengeance. You want his childhood, his future, his life to be clouded by your hatred?"

"Well I—"

"You want to pass that to your grandchildren?" I'll shake my head. "You know, this is why God told us to let Him take care of the vengeance. I'm not saying what the other guy did to you was right. I'm not saying it can be ignored. I'm saying you need to leave it up to God. If you don't leave it up to Him, if you get caught in this cycle of vengeance, it will haunt you for the rest of your life. You will just add to what this guy already has done to you. Is that what you want? You want what he did to inflict more damage on you? To your children? To your marriage?"

"Well, no, but—"

"Then leave it up to God. In fact, the worst thing you can do to him is be nice to him. If he has a conscience at all, God will pour emotional coals of fire on his head."

It may take some convincing because this Fallen Christian type can become consumed with vengeance and hate. It is important to explain the biblical aspects of forgiveness. Forgiveness is not for the person who did the wrong; it is for the person wronged. We are to forgive so we can rid ourselves of the bitterness that will destroy our spirits and endanger our own relationships.

Forgiveness does not make a wrong right. It allows the wronged to move beyond the wrong and to give himself a chance to enjoy life without having to live in the shadow of an injustice.

Step 5a: Help Them Through the Healing Process

An injustice, rightly or wrongly, leaves a wound in the emotional and spiritual psyche of an individual. The Bible is fairly clear that we are to help such injured Christians through the healing process.

> ***James 5:16** — Confess your faults one to another, and pray one for another, that ye may be healed. The effectual fervent prayer of a righteous man availeth much.*

As already mentioned, prayer is an essential ingredient in the success of the healing process. Help him through the injustice. Give him a different perspective and direction. Provide a light of Jesus Christ for him to latch onto.

Restoring This Fallen Christian in the Post-Vengeance Phase

After a person has sought his vengeance, he will come to learn that he has committed a travesty against his own spirit and injured his own relationships. Absalom ended up a hunted man, fled to a foreign country, and left behind everything he held dear to him—including his sister. So too shall the Fallen Christian discover similar spiritual and emotional pain after he seeks his vengeance.

However, this person is not too difficult to restore, assuming that the Christian has the spiritual strength to make the effort. In short, this person needs two things to be restored:

1. Forgiveness
2. Acceptance

David didn't give these things to Absalom, and Absalom eventually went out and tried to overthrow him. It was Joab who brought Absalom home after three years, not David. After two years of living next door and not being allowed to see his own father, Absalom forced Joab to take him to David.

David, however, gave him the cold shoulder (2 Samuel 14:25–33). The kiss David gave Absalom was more of a dismissal, not a greeting. David didn't forgive Absalom for his murder of Amnon, nor did he accept Absalom. All this after forgiving Amnon his rape of Tamar! No doubt Absalom seethed with injustice, bitterness, and resentment.

With even more confirmation—at least in the mind of Absalom—of the broken system, he went out immediately and began to conspire against his father—much like he had against Amnon (2 Samuel 15:1–6). It was all about betrayal and justice to Absalom. He felt that the king's justice was a hoax and a fraud. His hatred for Amnon now became hatred for his father. David came to regret his actions later (2 Samuel 18:33).

Don't allow the Fallen Christian to believe he can't be forgiven or accepted. Ironically, these are the same two things he refused to give to the person on whom he sought vengeance. But then sin never makes much sense. Here are some things you can do to help restore this Christian back to the loving embrace of Jesus Christ.

Step 1b: Pray for Him

Prayer is just as important in this phase as it was in the last one. You need guidance and wisdom. You need to be able to approach such a Fallen Christian without bitterness or resentment in your own heart.

Being a Restorer without enlisting God's aid is like a carpenter without any tools or a car with no gas. Prayer works.

Step 2b: Forgive and Accept Him

If he has already acted on his hatred, he needs to be forgiven and accepted. Forgive where he would not forgive and accept him when he would not accept another. The cycle of vengeance and hatred needs to be broken. Let God take care of the injustices. Focus, instead, on breaking the cycle.

Too many Fallen Christians are lost when we look at the evil things they have done and we play judge, jury, and executioner. We condemn them to others, condemn them in our hearts, condemn them in our actions and in the words we say, and condemn them from our fellowship. Let me ask you: how does this further the cause of Christ?

Thank God someone could forgive and accept the Apostle Paul. Thank God for Barnabas. Otherwise, we might have lost the greatest Christian who ever lived. Thank God someone left vengeance to God and simply forgave and accepted. This is what we need to do for this Christian. I'm aware that some circumstances may mean a particular Christian ought to leave a particular church or even wind up in jail. But that does not mean there is no longer any place for him in Christianity. Send him to the loving and accepting embrace of a fellow body of believers if need be, but don't exile him!

The couple of times I recommended that someone leave our church, it was only because I felt my ability to help them had been frustrated or their previous actions had created an atmosphere of tension and uneasiness that others could not pass over. We looked for and found a church they could become a part of, where they could gain the healing and acceptance they needed.

Other than that, you should do everything in your power to forgive and accept.

Step 3b: Ignoring the Problem Will Make Things Worse

If left alone or ignored, this type of Fallen Christian will simply shift their hatred and sense of injustice to entirely new targets. Neither you nor your church needs that level of turmoil. Don't ignore him.

David ignored his son Absalom after his return home. This only frustrated Absalom more until he finally made his father the target of his hatred. Be aware of the Fallen Christian's sensitivity to acceptance. He needs to be included. He needs to be given time to see the errors of his ways and to seek to repair the damage he has done.

Only those who find acceptance and forgiveness usually seek to repair any damage done in their quest for vengeance. Give them that chance!

Step 4b: Give Him Opportunity to Make It Right

If he makes any attempt to make amends, you have to jump on it. Punishing someone who feels like he did what is right will not help. You must allow time to demonstrate to him the foolishness of his hatred and the evil of his actions. You must give God the chance to change his heart.

When the decision is made to make amends, help him. Don't sit back and watch. I've had many people come to me with a heavy heart because of guilt of some action done in the past. In most cases, I assist them in making amends. I have written many letters for people who just don't know how to word things. I have made phone calls on behalf of people. I have made personal visits with those seeking to get things right.

It is amazing how much a person can be persuaded to do the right thing if they know they don't have to do it alone!

Step 5b: Don't Let Him Run Without Resistance

Absalom ran from his father's wrath, wrath he felt was completely unjustified when seen in the light of David's inaction regarding Amnon. Once away from his father, he spent three years in exile; David made no attempt to get him back. None. Absolutely none. Joab could see that David wanted Absalom back, but that David was unwilling to do anything about it. It was Joab who talked David into sending for his son. This became very apparent to Absalom.

Rejection, betrayal, and injustice fueled Absalom's hatred. Forgiveness and acceptance would have smothered it. David's inability to reach out to his son cost him his son.

Reach out to this type of Fallen Christian. Only under the embrace of acceptance and forgiveness will they have the ability to let go of their hatred and bitterness. Only then will they seek to make any amends that can be made.

A Word to This Type of Fallen Christian

If you fall into this category of fallen Christian, then you are either seeking vengeance or you have already done so. If you are seeking it, be warned—this is a sovereign power of God. You have no right to seek vengeance on your own.

With that in mind, let me be clear about some things regarding the wrong done to you or someone you know. It is not fair. Worse, you may have to live with the consequences of someone else's evil. That's not fair either. I am not asking you to accept what was done. I am not asking that you ignore it or the consequences of it. I am not asking that you take the person who did the wrong out to a steak dinner, clap him on the back, and go watch a ball game together. I'm not even asking that you trust him.

I am asking that you leave vengeance up to God.

The focus can't be on what the other fellow did wrong, but on what you can do right. Vengeance only begets vengeance. Systems break and people fail. It is not fair. But your relationship with God and with those around you must become your focus. Absalom became so consumed with anger over the injustice inflicted on his sister that his actions severed his relationship with her when he fled the country. How did that help Tamar?

I'm not asking you to pretend everything is okay. I'm just asking that you give it to God to deal with.

Remember, if it was you on the other side of the equation and you wanted to make it right, but no one would let you, how would you feel? God is better at this than you are. It is not your job. And it is never worth it.

12

King Nebuchadnezzar's Fall – Pride

Text to Study: Daniel 4

Characteristics and Signs of This Fallen Type

1. Is filled with pride.
2. Will ignore the dangers and warning signs of his imminent fall.
3. Is caught up in what he has accomplished.
4. Likes to brag.
5. Thinks his talents and skills give him the right to possess something or be something.
6. Is often critical of other people and their achievements.
7. Likes attention and being the focus.

Why Did King Nebuchadnezzar Fall?

The better question is more aptly, why did God humble King Nebuchadnezzar? You can make the case that Ol' Nebby didn't really fall. In one sense, his pride is clear proof that he did fall, but he didn't fall into a sin per se or follow any of the patterns that have been discussed in this book so far. His heart was simply lifted up in pride—arguably the worst sin—and God humbled him.

> ***Daniel 4:4*** *– I Nebuchadnezzar was at rest in mine house, and flourishing in my palace:*
>
> ***Daniel 4:30*** *– The king spake, and said, Is not this great Babylon, that I have built for the house of the kingdom by the might of my power, and for the honour of my majesty?*

Ol' Nebby was the king of the world's most powerful empire. Although, as far as empires go, his was a rather small one in terms of landmass, he still ruled the most developed region on earth. In this respect, he had a worldwide empire and left an indelible mark on history. Having secured a vast empire (at least in terms of the times), he looked upon everything his hands had accomplished and his heart filled with pride.

God had a point to prove to the man who would rule the Jews. Three times in Daniel chapter 4, God made a very direct and overt point to Nebuchadnezzar:

> ***Daniel 4:17*** *– This matter is by the decree of the watchers, and the demand by the word of the holy ones: to the intent that the living may know that the most High ruleth in the kingdom of men, and giveth it to whomsoever he will, and setteth up over it the basest of men.*
>
> ***Daniel 4:25*** *– That they shall drive thee from men, and thy dwelling shall be with the beasts of the field, and they shall make thee to eat grass as oxen, and they shall wet thee with the dew of heaven, and seven times shall pass over thee, till thou know that the most High ruleth in the kingdom of men, and giveth it to whomsoever he will.*
>
> ***Daniel 4:32*** *– And they shall drive thee from men, and thy dwelling shall be with the beasts of the field: they shall*

> *make thee to eat grass as oxen, and seven times shall pass over thee, until thou know that the most High ruleth in the kingdom of men, and giveth it to whomsoever he will.*

For all of Ol' Nebby's power and might, God allowed insanity to strike him. For seven years, the most powerful man on earth lived like a rabid beast. Imagine waking up from a seven-year stretch of insanity and remembering all seven years! No wonder Nebuchadnezzar said at the last:

> **Daniel 4:37** – *Now I Nebuchadnezzar praise and extol and honour the King of heaven, all whose works are truth, and his ways judgment: and those that walk in pride he is able to abase.*

Pride in authority is incredibly dangerous, because when he is humbled, it impacts so many other people. Pride in anyone's life is a sure way to be set up for a fall.

Outward Signs to Look For

1. *His pride is self-absorbed.* Everyone struggles with pride, but in the case of this Fallen Christian, he is hyper aware of his accomplishments, skills, talents, popularity, strengths, and power. He revels in it. He is in love with himself, so to speak.

2. *He is often critical or resentful of others.* Pride does not take competition well. It wants to be the only king on any hill. So he will criticize and even attack others whom he sees as being in direct competition to him.

3. *He craves for the spotlight to be on him.* He needs constant affirmation of his power or abilities. He seeks praise and adoration.

4. *He will be humbled.* This is almost like a universal natural law. God resists the proud (James 4:6, 1 Peter 5:5). Something will come along to humble him. It could be something as simple as old age to a man proud of his physical prowess. Either way, he will be humbled in some form.

How to Restore This Type of Fallen Christian

Step 1: Pray for Him

At the expense of sounding like a broken record, prayer works. Prayer is vital. Pride is such a consuming problem. It literally fills a person's heart. The best way to combat that is to labor in prayer for such a Fallen Christian. You must keep in mind your goal here. God will eventually humble this individual, but you can't rejoice in it when it happens. You need to be on hand to restore him.

Step 2: Warn Him of the Dangers of His Pride

This is an important step, but not everyone is in a position to do it. God sent Nebuchadnezzar a dream to warn him of his pride (Daniel 4:5–27). But only God was in a position to do this. No one else had the power, respect, or position to warn the most powerful man on the earth.

When a Fallen Christian is filled with pride, he will not listen to anyone he consciously or unconsciously deems as inferior to himself. He will only—possibly—listen to someone whom he respects or feels has already achieved what he is working to get.

In this regard, a role model is actually in the best position to do the warning. A person becomes a role model when he is picked by the one emulating him. You can't choose to be a role model for someone; to become one, someone must choose you to be a role model. If you are the role model for this particular Christian, then you need to warn him of the dangers of his pride. If you are not the role model, enlist the help of whoever is, if possible.

Privately take this Fallen Christian aside and have a long talk with him about where you see his pride taking him. Explain in as much detail as possible the dangers he is facing. Give him specific examples of other people as well as some from his own life.

Step 3: Be Genuine in Your Concern

Scripture tells us that when Daniel heard the dream, he was literally stunned into silence for a solid hour (Daniel 4:19). Daniel truly cared. His eyes didn't light up in glee at the thought of the enslavers of his people acting like a beast. He didn't praise God. He didn't run off to tell his friends in delicious detail about Ol' Nebby's fall. No, Daniel was genuinely concerned.

If your concern isn't genuine, your words will come through as pretentious and hypocritical. Does the plight of your friend drive you to labor in prayer? Do you weep for him? Does your heart feel like it is going to be swallowed up by your stomach? Do you really care?

If you read Daniel's words (Daniel 4:19–27), you will get a sense that Daniel loved Nebuchadnezzar. He tried, really tried, to help.

Your words need the backing of your heart to be effective. If you don't care, you won't make the difference you want to make. Restoring a Fallen Christian isn't about showing people how good you are at it (pride), it is about bringing him back to the loving embrace of Jesus Christ.

Step 4: Be There for Him When He Is Humbled

If you haven't been able to get him to turn around by this time, then he will be humbled. I can't say when. I can't tell you how. I just know it will happen. When it does, be there for him.

After Nebuchadnezzar suffered seven years of insanity, his reason came back to him (Daniel 4:36). When that happened, his friends and people sought him out. People were there for him. They did not take advantage of his absence to usurp him, make fun of him, or rejoice in his plight. No, they helped him back.

Someone needs to do this too. I have no doubt in my mind that when Nebuchadnezzar walked back into the city, sane and in his right mind, he felt embarrassed. Being humbled is embarrassing! But when he was accepted back, his mind and words praised God instead of himself. He became a true servant of God.

A Word to This Type of Fallen Christian

Pride is a sneaky problem. We all suffer it. We all deal with it. Somehow even revel in it. You may be this Fallen Christian. You may really think you are better than anyone else. You may believe you deserve certain things. You may think you are entitled to adulation, praise, or popularity. You may even crave these things.

But then, most likely, you don't think in those terms. You don't see your pride as others see it. It takes a lot of self-introspection to recognize pride. If you really want to know—and following the steps below will most likely be a humbling experience—then do the following:

1. Choose three role models, people whom you admire and whose admiration you crave.

2. Go to each of them separately and ask them to honestly evaluate your pride. Do not interrupt. Do not argue. Do not disagree. Just listen. Just take it all in.

3. Ask them if they foresee any dangers in your life due to your decisions, desires, or pride. Listen to their words carefully. Take it at face value and don't resist, justify, or qualify.

4. Go to your knees privately and bring their words to God. Ask God if they are right. Ask Him how to change. Humble yourself before God humbles you.

This last point is the key. If you humble yourself first, then God doesn't have to. This is always the best result.

James 4:10 *– Humble yourselves in the sight of the Lord, and he shall lift you up.*

> ***1 Peter 5:6** – Humble yourselves therefore under the mighty hand of God, that he may exalt you in due time:*

Humbling yourself is something every Christian should do on a regular basis. This is the best way to avoid being humbled by God. The latter always seems to be more dramatic and traumatic than the former.

Please, before your pride consumes you, give the points listed above a shot.

13

Samson's Fall – Played the Fool

Text to Study: Judges 14–16

Characteristics and Signs of This Fallen Type

1. Is careless and purely reactionary.
2. Tends to follow the path of least resistance.
3. Is mouthy and can't control his tongue.
4. Is quick to anger.
5. Has a blatant disregard for authority and advice.
6. Fits the Biblical description of a fool.

Why Did Samson Fall?

Primarily, Samson fell because he was a careless man who looked to follow the path of least resistance. He never thought before he acted. He took what he saw and didn't listen to any other reasoning.

Look at some of Samson's decisions:

1. *Judges 14:1–3* – He saw a woman. He wanted her. He demanded that his father get her for him and would not listen to his father's advice. God used Samson's impulsiveness, but it brought Samson nothing but trouble.

2. *Judges 14:9* – He broke his Nazarite vow of not coming close to anything dead. He saw honey within a lion's carcass. He wanted it. He took it. He had no thought of the consequences. As far as we know, he never even thought twice about breaking his vow.

3. *Judges 14:12* – The riddle to his new wife's friends is another example of his impulsiveness. He was poking fun at these guys and apparently never gave a thought to what they might do. In the end, he killed thirty men to honor the wager, and his wife was given to a man he'd hired to be his friend. Crazy. (There exists a strong possibility, though it can't be proven, that he drank wine at this feast to blend in with the other young men. If so, then he broke the part of the Nazarite vow of not touching anything associated with the grape.)

4. *Judges 15:1–2* – Samson returned to his wife—whom he had ignored for months—only to find out she was now married to another man. He reacted in typical Samson fashion: he burned down the wheat fields. This action also cost his wife her life. The Philistines killed her and her family for provoking Samson. Samson then went off and killed his wife's murderers out of revenge. His rage and unthinking reactions only succeeded in creating more trouble. Well done, Samson! Again, God used Samson's actions to eventually free Israel from the yoke of Philistine rule, but Samson's own life was a total shambles.

5. *Judges 15:11* – His actions nearly cost the families of Judah their lives. In fear for their lives, they bound Samson and turned him over to the Philistines. Samson went on a

rampage, killing his Philistine captors. Samson succeeded in making himself rather friendless, even among his own people. His actions weren't those of a liberator, but those of an arrogant, selfish, and prideful man.

6. *Judges 15:17–18* – He changed the name of the city or place of Lehi twice in the space of mere minutes, due to his ever-shifting emotions and spontaneous outbursts.

7. *Judges 16:1–2* – He broke the third part of the Nazarite vow of keeping himself clean by lying with a harlot. He saw. He took. It was as simple as that for Samson. He always took the path of least resistance.

8. *Judges 16:4* – Not to be outdone, he fell in love with another woman who was an unbeliever, Delilah. This wasn't some Hebrew girl who loved the same God he purported to follow; rather, this was a woman addicted to money. Her interest in Samson was the money he would bring her.

9. *Judges 16:16* – When this harlot became a constant nag, seeking the source of his strength, he simply gave in, taking the path of least resistance. That was the story of his life. He ended up breaking the last part of his Nazarite vow when Delilah cut off his hair. He became enslaved, his eyes were gouged out, and he was mocked.

To sum up Samson's life with one word, I would choose "fool." We all know Christians like this. They may even be among the most common types of Fallen Christians. It is a matter of simple foolishness and little to no wisdom. Samson made a mess of his life, and the Christian who has Samson-like tendencies usually messes his life up too.

Samson didn't set out to mess up his life. He just saw, acted, and reacted. This is typical foolish behavior. His own foolish decisions led him to the sorry state he eventually found himself in. This wasn't Cain, who tried to do right and felt rejected for it. This wasn't Absalom, seeking vengeance for an injustice. This wasn't

Peter, who felt guilty after his betrayal of Christ. This wasn't David, trying to hide his sin. This wasn't even King Saul, seeking to justify his actions. This was a fool. He was like a pinball bouncing here and there with no real direction in life.

Outward Signs to Look For

A fool is simply someone who allows his passions, lusts, and desires to choose the path he walks.

1. *He doesn't wonder about the consequences of his actions. He just acts out of pure desire.*

2. *He usually takes the path of least resistance with no regard for the destination.* If it looks good, then that is all he desires to know.

3. *His current emotions become his guide to decision making. Everything is spur of the moment.* No plan. No thought. Just pure action on lustful desires.

4. *He rarely thinks of others… is mostly selfish.*

5. *He usually believes he is the exception to the rule.* Samson had superior strength from God, so he figured he was invincible. The fool usually never thinks bad things will happen to him.

6. *He will often repeat blunders because he believes the first one was merely bad luck or wasn't his fault.* He returns to his own folly.

7. *He rarely knows the depth of trouble he is in (Judges 16:20).* He isn't just ignorant; he intentionally rejects wisdom.

8. *He does have access to the right path; he just believes his is better.* So he blindly blows ahead, thinking that no matter what has happened to others who have walked this path, it won't happen to him.

9. *He may not even be a God-hater (Samson wasn't); he is just interested in going a different way.*

10. *He may even love Christianity, but he believes himself to be the exception to the rule.*

11. *He simply follows a path chosen by his desires and passions.*

Proverbs 12:15 – *The way of a fool is right in his own eyes: but he that hearkeneth unto counsel is wise.*

Out of 78 verses in Proverbs that use the word "fool" or "foolishness," 21 of those times are about how a fool uses his tongue!

Here is the list of verses from Proverbs: 9:13, 10:8, 10:10, 10:14, 10:18, 12:23, 14:3, 14:7, 14:9, 14:16, 15:2, 15:7, 15:14, 17:7, 17:28, 18:6, 18:7, 19:1, 26:7, 26:9, 29:11, and 29:20.

You spot a fool by how he uses his tongue. A fool can't help but wag the ol' tongue. Just listen to what comes out of a person's mouth, and you'll quickly discover whether he's a fool.

How to Restore This Type of Fallen Christian

Step 1: Pray for Him

Prayer is still a very much-needed part of any restoration. So keep on praying. Dealing with this type of Fallen Christian will be extremely exasperating. Prayer will help you keep your focus.

Step 2: He Must Come to See Himself as a Fool

He must reach a point where the pain from his decisions causes him to realize that he needs to do things different. For Samson, his actions and decisions may have consumed twenty years of his adult life. Only at the last, beaten, blinded, and all alone, did he bow himself before God. His end decision got him into the Hall of Faith of Hebrews 11, but it came at the expense of his life. To be frank, I wouldn't want anyone to have to go to that extreme to realize how foolish he has been.

The choices we make as children and teenagers often set the tone for our lives for the next 20–30 years. Interestingly enough, many people don't see themselves having played the fool until they reach their middle years. We see this manifested in what is known as a midlife crisis.

The fool goes through two mental and highly destructive stages before he finally comes to accept that he is a fool or has been playing the fool.

1. He believes all his problems are just bad luck. He is convinced that next time will be different. He will continue to do the same things, believing there is happiness to be found in it. When he doesn't get it. He just thinks it is bad luck. He will do it again!

2. He comes to believe that it isn't bad luck, but people who are out to get him. If it wasn't for so and so, then none of this would have happened! If so and so hadn't gotten involved, I wouldn't be in trouble!

Many people have to go through these two stages before they finally realize that the common denominator in all their problems is themselves! For many, they must be willing to accept responsibility for their own actions before you can restore them. It may take years for a person to get to this point.

Step 3: You Must Drive His Foolishness from Him

If you have enough influence, it is possible to restore this type of Fallen Christian by driving his foolishness from him. First, however, you need to understand the nature of the fool as the Bible explains it. Here are some foolish qualities to be on the lookout for:

1. *Present Wrath* (Proverbs 12:16 – A fool's wrath is presently known: but a prudent man covereth shame.) – Yep, Samson's wrath was certainly something he didn't hold back. If things didn't go exactly the way he felt they should, he got angry and let his anger do something right then.

Watch for this. People who are quickly angry are exhibiting foolish traits. Quick anger is evidence of a selfish and prideful personality. People who give some thought to other perspectives are rarely prone to quick anger.

2. *Foolish Rage and Foolish Confidence* (Proverbs 14:16 – A wise man feareth, and departeth from evil: but the fool rageth, and is confident.) – Samson raged when things didn't go his way. He was confidently wrong. Many fools, when they are wrong, are incapable of seeing it. They are confident that this time things will turn out different. Ever tried to talk someone out of a foolish choice, but their unfounded confidence in their own invulnerability became a wall to your wisdom and guidance? It is difficult to change the course of a fool even when it is so obviously an act of foolishness.

3. *Despises Instruction and Reproof* (Proverbs 15:5 – A fool despiseth his father's instruction: but he that regardeth reproof is prudent.) – Samson consistently ignored his parent's advice and instructions. He violated his parent's promise that Samson would remain a Nazarite from his birth. People who cavalierly ignore advice from parents, elders, and authority do so because they are fools. A great indicator of foolishness and wisdom is how someone handles advice. If the only thing he wants to hear is what he wants to do, than most likely he is a fool.

4. *His Mouth Constantly Gets Him into Trouble* (Proverbs 18:6 – A fool's lips enter into contention, and his mouth calleth for strokes.) – Samson consistently looked to get into conflict. His mouth often got him into trouble. Yes, I think it is clear, Samson was a fool. Perhaps the easiest way to identify a fool is by the words that come out of their mouths. Without realizing it, a fool will brand himself a

fool in the eyes of those around him. Without understanding it, a fool will proclaim his foolishness.

Once you have determined, biblically, that a person is acting the fool, you need to attack those areas that demonstrate his foolish qualities. You may have to confront him regarding his anger, his tongue, his authority issues, and his refusal to take advice. Until he can come to believe that he is the problem, he won't see a problem.

Step 4: Refocus His Desires on a Different Path

If you can find someone who can demonstrate to him that the way he is going will result in pain, loss, or the inability to gain what he wants, he may choose to go another way.

This is easiest to accomplish while he is yet a child. Foolishness is bound in the heart of a child, but it can be driven far from him. In the case of an adult, it is much more difficult. He may not even listen to reason.

Proverbs 22:15 *– Foolishness is bound in the heart of a child; but the rod of correction shall drive it far from him.*

See also Proverbs 13:24, 19:18, 23:13–14, 29:15, and 17.

Proverbs 26:3 *– A whip for the horse, a bridle for the ass, and a rod for the fool's back.*

It is true that many people who are fools realize the errors of their ways when they get hurt. Bailing them out of trouble is one of the worst things you can do. Many parents, who continually bail their children out of problems, never let their children discover the consequences of their own actions. This costs the children. Samson had the superior strength to bail himself out of any physical retribution, so he never cared.

The problem with never suffering consequences is that it creates a lack of desire to change. Either this Fallen Christian hasn't reached the point where he is willing to blame his problems on himself, or he hasn't been hurt enough to shake himself from his own foolish notions.

> ***Proverbs 17:10*** *– A reproof entereth more into a wise man than an hundred stripes into a fool.*
>
> ***Proverbs 27:22*** *– Though thou shouldest bray a fool in a mortar among wheat with a pestle, yet will not his foolishness depart from him.*

Step 5: Teach Him to Control His Tongue

Your ability to control your tongue is the greatest key in your ability to control your passions, desires, and lusts (James 1:26). The tongue can't be tamed (James 3:8), but it can be controlled. If you put it in a cage, place guards around it, then you have just developed the means to control the other things in your life. The tongue is the hardest part of our anatomy to control—and it can never be tamed. You must always be on guard, never trust it. Teach this to the Fallen Christian you are ministering to.

James 3:2 teaches us that the ability to control the tongue makes us a balanced person. Whereas immaturity is often bound up in a loose tongue, maturity is often reflected in a controlled tongue. James 3:6 teaches us that the tongue leads to the nature of hell.

Proverbs 17:28 tells us that if a fool can restrain his tongue, he will be counted wise. Interesting. Once again, we see the clear lines of maturity drawn in that verse. James 1:19 tells us to be slow to speak and swift to hear—elements again of maturity.

Control of the tongue means you will listen more. You will hear more. You will consider more. You will understand more. You will be wiser.

> ***Proverbs 29:20*** *– Seest thou a man that is hasty in his words? there is more hope of a fool than of him.*

> ***Proverbs 26:12*** *– Seest thou a man wise in his own conceit? there is more hope of a fool than of him.*

A Christian who cannot control his tongue will remain a fool. He has to place his ego and pride under tight control. Only by doing that can he rein in the tongue. Once our pride is injured or we get a bruised ego, our tongue begins to wag. This is incredibly dangerous. It is necessary to learn to put a firm rein on that pride and ego. This is something that can be taught.

Restoring this type of Fallen Christian can be a frustrating process. You may find yourself having to pick up the pieces of his shattered life to restore him.

A Word to This Type of Fallen Christian

A quick check to see if you are playing the fool yourself is to look at three things:

1. Do you feel that the bad things that happen in your life over and over again are merely bad luck?
2. Do you feel that if it weren't for certain people in your life, you would be in a much better place?
3. Do you struggle controlling your tongue?

If you answered "yes" to any of them, then you may be playing the fool. Merely reading this is not sufficient to get you to see that, however. Already you are justifying in your mind why a "yes" to any of the three questions is actually a good thing. And that's the point.

I would like to propose a challenge to you. Go one single day without saying a single negative thing about anyone. Go one single day without voicing your opinion on anything. The point of this exercise is not to get you to control your tongue—most everyone does these things every day—but to get you to see how much you are doing it every day.

It may shock you.

14

The Apostate's Fall – Apostasy and Rejection

Text to Study: Hebrews 6:1–9

Characteristics and Signs of This Fallen Type

1. Once believed, but has rejected his own beliefs.
2. Rejected the teachings of the Bible he once trusted, taught, believed, and followed.
3. Is vocal and active in his denial.
4. Is usually angry at Christianity or God.
5. Cannot be reasoned with.
6. Will twist anything said from the Bible.

Why Did the Apostate Fall?

By definition, an apostate is someone who once believed, but has chosen to reject his own beliefs. He has chosen to reject everything he once held dear, once trusted in, once believed.

The reasons for this are as varied as those who become apostates. But any of the other eleven types described in preceding chapters can become an apostate if there is no Restorer to help bring them back. When there is no Restorer, the individual in question will have his faith shaken. If it is shaken strongly enough or his treatment by other Christians is harsh enough, he may become an apostate.

Many people become what I call denomination apostates. These are people who switch religions or denominations because of some crisis, treatment, or being disenfranchised in some way. Others will go to the more extreme of rejecting anything even remotely associated with religion of any kind.

Any of the fallen types so far discussed in this book can lead to apostasy. I believe this can only happen if there is no Restorer to reach out to them. If someone would have been there when their faith was shaken, they would have gotten past it.

Outward Signs to Look For

There is no clear example of a person in Scripture who believed and then rejected Christ as a total belief system. Paul wrote of Demas, who forsook him because of his love of the world—but that doesn't hint that Demas rejected his belief in Christ totally, rather that he chose the world over Christ (2 Timothy 4:10).

The only thing we really have is a description of such a person given in Hebrews 6. The beginning of Hebrews 6 is a very, very controversial passage. I believe that I have read or heard at least a score of different opinions that range from losing your salvation to the belief that the passage only refers to the nation of Israel's rejection of Christ as the Messiah.

So I might as well throw my own two cents worth in. I'll try to be logical in my approach, and I think you'll at the very least see my point.

I believe the passage deals with backslidden and Fallen Christians—specifically apostates. There is a key here that the Restorer needs to understand when setting out to restore a Fallen Christian: some fallen ones, though they can come back, will not be restored by you or any other Christian!

Let's look at the verses:

> ***Hebrews 6:1–9*** *– Therefore leaving the principles of the doctrine of Christ, let us go on unto perfection; not laying again the foundation of repentance from dead works, and of faith toward God, Of the doctrine of baptisms, and of laying on of hands, and of resurrection of the dead, and of eternal judgment. And this will we do, if God permit. For it is impossible for those who were once enlightened, and have tasted of the heavenly gift, and were made partakers of the Holy Ghost, And have tasted the good word of God, and the powers of the world to come, If they shall fall away, to renew them again unto repentance; seeing they crucify to themselves the Son of God afresh, and put him to an open shame. For the earth which drinketh in the rain that cometh oft upon it, and bringeth forth herbs meet for them by whom it is dressed, receiveth blessing from God: But that which beareth thorns and briers is rejected, and is nigh unto cursing; whose end is to be burned. But, beloved, we are persuaded better things of you, and things that accompany salvation, though we thus speak.*

Again, the Bible speaks, in my opinion, of a Christian who falls away, of a Christian who intentionally and deliberately turns his back on the truth of the Bible, even his belief in God, and perhaps anything to do with God. He has become an apostate. We've all met someone like this. Usually, they are bitter and angry people. Any time the topic of God, or church, or Christianity is brought up, they become hyper angry or calloused.

I do not think that the passage is referring to the loss of salvation either. Many people have taken it that way, but that is not the message here. Repentance doesn't necessarily mean salvation. God, Himself, repented (Exodus 32:14). Repentance is a change of mind, a deliberate act that changes the course of your thinking or actions.

I believe it teaches that once a person who knows the truth intentionally turns his back on it, he has made it is impossible for another Christian to change his mind back. No debate, no argument, no logic will renew him to his original state. He's already been there, done that, got the t-shirt, so to speak. What argument could possibly persuade someone who has already decided that anything based on the Bible or Christianity is by default false?

It doesn't mean he can't come back. It just means other Christians won't be able to reason him back.

I meet them around town. Every argument, no matter how sound, is dismissed by someone who used to be an avid church-goer, perhaps even a former preacher. He's already heard all the sermons before, had once held to the truth, and now chooses to reject it. I can't make any headway when someone who has heard it all before has already rejected the truth I am trying to highlight.

If you study the passage, you will notice that the object of the passage is "those" and the subject is "us." It is trying to teach us that we can't renew those who fall away once they have tasted of the heavenly gift. Before they taste, we can share with them the truth of the Gospel and witness to them about Jesus Christ. They may repent from their old beliefs and turn instead to Jesus for salvation. But if they do that, and later turn back away from it, we won't be able to use the old arguments that worked the first time.

This idea is established at the beginning of the passage as well.

Hebrews 6:1–3 *– Therefore leaving the principles of the doctrine of Christ, let us go on unto perfection; not laying again the foundation of repentance from dead works, and of faith toward God, Of the doctrine of baptisms, and of laying on of hands, and of resurrection of the dead, and of eternal judgment. And this will we do, if God permit.*

They were arguing over fundamentals with each other. Some had apparently changed their stance, and this caused a massive debate and argument. Paul, assuming he wrote the book of Hebrews, told them to stop that nonsense. He told them they wouldn't be able to argue back into the fold those who changed their position. He told them that they needed to go on and grow.

You've met them. Try and argue someone back to Christianity who has been taught all the things you have and then chooses to leave it anyway. You'll not get anywhere.

A very loving couple in our church had a friend who had surrendered to God's will to preach, was an avid church attender, a prayer warrior, and a wonderful soul winner until he abruptly turned his back on the whole thing. They tried to reach out to him by quoting Scriptures and using the Bible to restore him. He only twisted the verses around and threw them back in their faces. He became antagonistic and aggressive toward Christians and blatantly refused anything that came from where he once was.

This type of Christian can't be restored by another Christian. It is impossible for us to renew them again to another change of their mind. It just won't happen.

How to Restore This Type of Fallen Christian

You can't restore him. So what can you do?

Step 1: Pray for Him

Pray for him. Love him. Be a friend when he needs it. Other than that, you can't do anything. Only God can break through his wall at this point.

We're not talking about a Christian who has just lost his way, or who fell into sin, or who allowed hatred or foolishness to dominate his heart. We're talking about someone who deliberately turned his back on Jesus Christ. We're talking about someone who has crucified Christ again and put Him to an open shame.

But that doesn't mean that he can't or won't ever come back. It just means you won't bring him back with your own words, persuasion, or influence. Still, there is always hope he can and will come back.

Step 2: Wait Until God Breaks Him

This usually means that God has to soften up a hard heart. The process could be very painful. God doesn't do this because He is angry, but rather because it is the only way to reach out to such a person. His heart must be brought to the place where he is willing to look for God again, and unfortunately, tragedy is usually the only way this can happen.

This is hard to wait for. As a pastor, I don't like to see anyone suffer. But if this person is going to come back, he will need to be broken first. As the Restorer, I try to prepare myself for this. I make sure that the Fallen Christian knows the door is open at any time. I don't attack, defame, or even preach a sermon about him. I make sure he knows that I am his friend.

And they do come back at times. When someone does, he is more like a Peter at that point. That is someone I can help restore.

Step 3: He Must Choose to Come Back on His Own

People do realize their mistakes—either through God's breaking or their own realization—and if they haven't burned every bridge behind them, they may seek to come back. The truth can dawn on them. They can realize the error of their ways. So be ready to receive them again if they decide to come back.

Outside of God's breaking, this is rare simply because of pride. Once you declare yourself against God, it is hard to say, "I was wrong. Sorry." The most dangerous hindrance to any spiritual growth, no matter who it is, is pride.

There is without doubt hope for such a Fallen Christian. But just understand that they won't be swayed by the persuasiveness of your arguments or the finesse of your logic. If they come back, it'll be because God somehow got a hold of their heart or they realized on their own the error they made.

You just need to be ready for when they do.

A Word to This Type of Fallen Christian

If you are this type of Fallen Christian, I can only conceive of two reasons why you are even reading this book. First, you were tricked or coerced into it as a favor to someone. Second, you were just curious what I would say about you.

I understand that nothing you read here will be convincing. You can't afford to let it be. Admitting you were wrong to leave Christianity would be such an appalling blow against your ego and pride that you can't afford to even entertain such a proposition. No one—and I don't care who they are, Christian or otherwise—likes to eat crow.

That doesn't mean, however, that there won't come a time when your faith—and yes, your lack of faith is an act of faith on your part—in whatever it is that you are now clinging to won't be challenged by God in some way. If at such a time, you believe you made a mistake in leaving Christianity, I for one will welcome you back with every bit of loving grace I can muster.

You won't even have to eat crow for me.

Your belief does not change the fact that God loves you, and He may not let you go without a fight.

PART TWO

Becoming Influential in the Life of the Fallen

Goals and Purpose of This Part of the Book

For the Restorer to be effective, he needs some measure of influence over the Fallen Christian he wishes to help restore. Without influence, your efforts will be wasted and your ability to help, limited. It is important that the Restorer learn to gain the right influence in order to be effective.

The following chapters will help the Restorer gain the needed influences to be effective in the life of the Fallen Christian. Study them well and then study the principles from God's Word thoroughly. Someone you love, someone you care about, someone you can help may need you to have enough influence in his life to help bring him back to the loving embrace of Jesus Christ.

Galatians 6:1 *– Brethren, if a man be overtaken in a fault, ye which are spiritual, restore such an one in the spirit of meekness; considering thyself, lest thou also be tempted.*

The command here is given to the spiritual Christian—to the Restorer. Come, let's do our job and do it effectively!

15

Understanding Motivations

Before we can venture into the area of influence, we need to understand motivation. All the persuasive power you possess will do you little good if you can't motivate someone to change. In the realm of restoring a Fallen Christian, the fallen one needs to have some motivation to come back. He needs to have a reason to change.

Many such individuals supply their own motivation to change, but you will want to understand what that motivation is. A Fallen Christian who wants to return to Jesus, who wants to get back in church, already has a motivation to do so. Your job as the Restorer is to understand what that motivation is and possibly add other motivations. Your influence on him will be greatly increased if you can understand his motivations.

No one does anything without some motivation. There exists some reason for what we do. It may not be something we can articulate. It may not be something we are consciously aware of. It may not even be something we like or enjoy. But some motivation does exist.

There are basically two types of motivations: negative and positive. The negative motivators are usually unsustainable simply because the motivation dies when we rid ourselves of a particular negative emotion or situation. Positive motivators are much more sustainable and often have longer-lasting results because we enjoy the effect and impact they have on our lives.

A List of Typical Negative Motivations

Fear of Loss

There is no greater motivation than this—I believe that includes love, despite the romantic in all of us. You could make the case that the fear of loss only achieves motivation because we love. We don't fear the loss of something we don't love or want. Nevertheless, the fear of loss is the most powerful of motivators.

The fear of loss has driven men to unusual extremes. On a small scale, it is the impetus for a fist fight on the playground, where phrases such as, "I saw it first! That's mine! Give it back to me!" are common. On a larger scale, it is the driving force behind arms races between nations.

***Hebrews 11:7** – By faith Noah, being warned of God of things not seen as yet, moved with fear, prepared an ark to the saving of his house; by the which he condemned the world, and became heir of the righteousness which is by faith.*

What was Noah's motivation to build the ark? Fear of loss. He didn't want to see his family die. No doubt he didn't want to die either. This fear of loss is often more powerful than love or compassion. Note the following verses:

***Jude 1:22–23** – And of some have compassion, making a difference: And others save with fear, pulling them out of the fire; hating even the garment spotted by the flesh.*

These verses speak of two different motivators: compassion and fear. It is understood here that if compassion doesn't motivate you, then perhaps the fear of loss might. Fear is a powerful motivator. Most of our more bizarre actions can be attributed to the fear of loss.

For the Fallen Christian, the fear of losing his marriage, his children, his job, his way of life, or his own health is often the motivation to come back to Christianity. The changes he makes are a direct response to his fear of loss. It happens over and over again. People come back to the Lord because they hope that by doing so they can keep whatever they fear losing.

Personally, I don't have a problem with this as a motivator to come back to Jesus Christ. After all, Christianity has real answers for real problems. However, it is a negative motivator. The problem with negative motivators is this: the motivation is often unsustainable because we seek to rid ourselves of the reason for the motivation—thus eliminating the motivation itself.

2 Timothy 1:7 – *For God hath not given us the spirit of fear; but of power, and of love, and of a sound mind.*

1 John 4:18 – *There is no fear in love; but perfect love casteth out fear: because fear hath torment. He that feareth is not made perfect in love.*

Love is a more sustainable motivator and should be the motivation that we want fear to translate into. The goal is not to live in fear, but to be free of fear. But, if the fear isn't translated into love, the motivation is gone when the fear is gone. When things turn around and begin going good again, I've seen many Christians slip right back into the mire of sin they were trying to climb out of. Some just lose interest because things start to go well, while others find their attraction to the world once again dominating their thinking.

The Children of Israel in the book of Judges are a good example of this type of motivator and the problems it can cause when it is no longer a motivation. When you read the book of Judges, you will quickly notice a pattern emerging. It goes something like this:

1. Things are going good; the people are prosperous.
2. The Children of Israel begin to slip into idolatry.
3. God warns them to repent. They refuse.
4. God sends judgment—usually an invading foreign power.
5. The people suffer. They begin losing things precious to them.
6. The people cry out to God for mercy. Their fear motivates them to come back.
7. God grants mercy.
8. Things begin to go good again. Prosperity returns.
9. The Children of Israel begin to slip back into idolatry.
10. The pattern repeats…

The Restorer must understand that if the fear of loss is a motivator, the motivation has a shelf life equal to the retention of the fear. When the fear is gone, so is the motivator. Unless there is another motivator to replace it, there is a very real possibility that the Christian may slip back.

Here is a list of things most of us fear to lose, and the fear of losing such can become powerful motivators in our lives:

1. Loss of life or limb.
2. Loss of a marriage.
3. Loss of family.
4. Loss of wealth or financial stability.
5. Loss of health.
6. Loss of prestige or popularity.
7. Loss of power.
8. Loss of possessions.
9. Loss of an important relationship.
10. Loss of a dream, ambition, or hope.

The Restorer ought to be aware of which fear is motivating the Fallen Christian. Knowing this may help you find an adequate replacement motivation when things begin to look up.

Jealousy

Jealousy is, like the last one, a negative motivator. It is also similar to the fear of loss in that, biblically speaking, jealousy is anger over the fear of losing something you believe to be your sole possession. Jealousy, therefore, is a combination of two negative motivators: fear of loss and anger.

***Deuteronomy 32:16** – They provoked him to jealousy with strange gods, with abominations provoked they him to anger.*

***Psalms 79:5** – How long, LORD? wilt thou be angry for ever? shall thy jealousy burn like fire?*

***Proverbs 6:34** – For jealousy is the rage of a man: therefore he will not spare in the day of vengeance.*

If you study the word "jealousy" in the Scriptures, you will notice that anger is almost universally associated with it. Here we have just three examples listed above. The first and second refer to God's jealousy as a result of His people turning away from Him and to strange gods. The last verse also tells a similar story. It is about a husband who discovers another man had slept with his wife. His jealousy, fear of losing something important to him, is accompanied by rage.

Usually, jealousy only motivates people to do rash, stupid things in a wild effort to win back what they believe is being stolen from them. In the case of a Fallen Christian, jealousy could have caused his fall, but it will only be a motivation to come back to the Lord when it becomes desperation.

He will have first tried everything else to keep what he fears he is losing and, when none of them work, he may try the Lord.

Again, this is a negative motivator that is rarely sustainable. Unless the Restorer can replace it with a positive motivator, this Fallen Christian will often revert back to his old ways in time.

Anger

It is rare that anger is a motivator to come back to God. But it can happen. It is a negative motivator and not very sustainable because most, again, are looking to arrive at a place where they don't have to be angry. Here are some reasons why anger may be a motivator to come back to the Lord.

1. Angry at the Devil and what he has done to him or his family.
2. Angry at the world and how it has turned on him or his family.
3. Angry at himself for bad or sinful decisions and actions.

The last one, anger at himself, is the most common of the three. I've dealt with many Fallen Christians who are just angry at themselves for falling. They hate themselves, what they have done, or where it took them. It is a form of guilty regret. They seek to chastise themselves in some way, to find some form of forgiveness and redemption.

This anger needs to be replaced by love. Love is a more sustainable motivator. The Restorer needs to realize that this Fallen Christian needs to have a different motivation. Anger either recedes or it builds to unmanageable levels. If it is not dealt with properly, they lose their motivation, or they are driven to do something incredibly hurtful.

A woman I knew came back to God because of her anger at herself for her behavior and actions. God forgave her. Our church rallied to her and forgave her. But she couldn't forgive herself. Her anger and guilty regret built to the point where she took her own life. If I could have seen the signs earlier, I might have been able to do something about it. But she kept it inward, bottled it up, and let it seethe in her heart.

Guilt

Guilt is a negative motivator that brings many Fallen Christians back to the Lord. A sense of betrayal, the weight of a sin burden can cause many a Fallen Christian to want to seek redemption and forgiveness. Again, I don't mind this. Anything that encourages a person to come back is good with me.

Guilt, in a way, is good. People who lack a conscious don't feel guilt. If a person feels guilt at all, that is a good sign. In fact, don't seek to alleviate their guilt too quickly. For some they never get a sense of peace unless they come to believe they've paid their debts.

***Hebrews 12:6–11** – For whom the Lord loveth he chasteneth, and scourgeth every son whom he receiveth. If ye endure chastening, God dealeth with you as with sons; for what son is he whom the father chasteneth not? But if ye be without chastisement, whereof all are partakers, then are ye bastards, and not sons. Furthermore we have had fathers of our flesh which corrected us, and we gave them reverence: shall we not much rather be in subjection unto the Father of spirits, and live? For they verily for a few days chastened us after their own pleasure; but he for our profit, that we might be partakers of his holiness. Now no chastening for the present seemeth to be joyous, but grievous: nevertheless afterward it yieldeth the peaceable fruit of righteousness unto them which are exercised thereby.*

A Fallen Christian may never find that peaceable fruit of righteousness if he doesn't feel he was in some way punished for his deed. Don't be too hasty to dismiss his guilt. Allow him to feel he has paid for his wrong in some way. In most cases, he just needs to know that someone believes in him and that he will be accepted back.

Even with children, one of the worst things that can happen to them is that they get away with doing wrong. Living with guilt is a poison. It needs to be purged, not ignored.

It is not the Restorer's job to punish or enact revenge. Your job for someone motivated by guilt is to help heal the wound, and help them find ways to repay their perceived debt. Once this happens, you will need to replace the guilt with a more positive motivation. Once the guilt is gone, often the motivation is gone as well. How many people do we know who stop doing something good because they believe a debt has been paid in full—they no longer need to do it?

Negative Desires

Desires such as envy, covetousness, and greed are motivators. It is rare indeed for a Fallen Christian to have one of these as a motivator to come back to the Lord. In most cases, where negative desires are motivators, it is not about Jesus Christ, but about another Christian they feel they are in competition with.

> ***3 John 1:9–10*** *— I wrote unto the church: but Diotrephes, who loveth to have the preeminence among them, receiveth us not. Wherefore, if I come, I will remember his deeds which he doeth, prating against us with malicious words: and not content therewith, neither doth he himself receive the brethren, and forbiddeth them that would, and casteth them out of the church.*

Here we see a negative desire motivating Diotrephes to refuse fellowship with the Apostles. It is indeed a rare thing to see a negative desire motivating a person to come back to the Lord.

The Restorer must be aware that there will be some who come in sheep's clothing, but they come back with a hidden agenda. Again, I cannot stress enough how important it is for the Restorer to be aware of the motivations in the life of a Fallen Christian you are trying to restore. The magnitude of your influence is dependent on understanding and then correctly utilizing the motivations in the life of the Fallen Christian.

Pride

Pride is a negative motivator because the motivations focus on self or self-gratification. Christians, out of pride, may try to look the part, read their Bible, say amen in church, and try to look good. Their pride may even be the dominant motivator in returning to Jesus Christ.

How can this be? It happens when a Christian wants to regain a particular image or a certain level of prestige he lost when he fell. Maybe he was a Sunday School teacher and lost his class. Maybe he was a popular preacher but lost that when he fell. Now, his pride wants it back. So he may attempt to come back out of pride. He may want to regain his former popularity or prestige.

This is a very dangerous motivator to use in trying to restore a Fallen Christian. All Christians coming back to Jesus need to see the relationship with Jesus as paramount—not a position, not popularity.

James 4:6 *– But he giveth more grace. Wherefore he saith, God resisteth the proud, but giveth grace unto the humble.*

There is no doubt that pride is a motivator. It usually leads people in the wrong way, however. The Restorer needs to be wary of such a motivator. If you are trying to help restore a Christian who is only interested in regaining lost popularity or position, there will be resistance by not only God, but from the person you are trying to help.

All your efforts will be viewed through the lenses of how well they assist in reviving his image.

A List of Typical Positive Motivations

Love

I speak not of being loved, but of loving as a proper, positive motivation. When a Fallen Christian returns due to his love for God, Christ, or the things of God, this is a motivation you can capitalize on and sustain.

Many Christians fall away during a momentary weakness. Their love for God, however, has not diminished. They will want to return.

They will want to come back. This I believe is the primary motivation behind Peter's restoration.

Three times in John 21, Jesus asked Peter if he loved Him. Peter did. Peter's love for Jesus had not diminished when he fell to a momentary weakness. And ultimately, it was his love for Jesus—more so than Jesus' love for Peter—that motivated Peter to come back to the Lord.

It is true that love is usually reciprocated. In other words, we love because we believe we are being loved.

1 John 4:19 – We love him, because he first loved us.

But love is a great motivator. We will go to unusual lengths for someone or something we love. If you, the Restorer, can cause a Fallen Christian to fall in love with Jesus Christ, they will have all the motivation they need to come back.

Seeking Acceptance or Being Loved

This is an important motivation. We, by nature, reciprocate love. Cast your mind back to grade school playground politics and recall the friendship offer you made to a fellow playmate: "I'll be your friend if you'll be mine." This type of reciprocation dominates our understanding of love. Why do children love their parents? Mostly it's because the parents loved them first. Why do we choose the friends we do? Mostly because we have witnessed some evidence of friendliness before committing to the friendship.

The Restorer must understand that this can be a powerful motivation. Being accepted is important. A Fallen Christian seeking restoration needs to feel there is some sort of acceptance from other Christians. They often refuse to make that first step until they see some evidence from fellow Christians that they would be accepted if they come back.

To some degree, this motivation to return to Jesus Christ after falling away is driven by a feeling of debt. When someone loves us, we reciprocate that love back as if we are paying off a debt. How many times do we feel obligated to have someone over to eat simply because they invited us over to eat first?

The Restorer can capitalize on this type of motivation by simply loving a Fallen Christian and accepting them back. Involving yourself in his life may produce a reciprocation that brings them closer and closer to Jesus Christ.

Purpose

This is one of the best motivators I can think of. Having a sense of purpose is essential to the restoration of a Fallen Christian. Purpose is a driving force that often accepts obstacles and then overcomes them. Many motivators fail upon the confrontation of an obstacle, but purpose will seek to overcome these obstacles.

> ***Daniel 1:8*** *– But Daniel purposed in his heart that he would not defile himself with the portion of the king's meat, nor with the wine which he drank: therefore he requested of the prince of the eunuchs that he might not defile himself.*

Daniel's purpose was the motivator to obey his God despite the immense pressure and even threat of death to do otherwise.

Athletes who have a purpose to win a race or competition will suffer many obstacles in their pursuit of their goal or purpose. People who have a purpose, a sense of duty and need, will tackle any obstacle.

For the Restorer, this is an ideal motivation. If you can help a Fallen Christian find purpose, his restoration will be almost ensured.

Positive Desires

We talked some of the negative desires, but there exist positive desires as well. Some have a desire to walk with God, to be blessed, to know God, to understand the mysteries of God, to serve God, and to fulfill God's will for their lives.

These desires are positive motivators.

> ***Proverbs 18:1*** *– Through desire a man, having separated himself, seeketh and intermeddleth with all wisdom.*

This is a great picture of a Fallen Christian who has the right desires to come back to the embrace of Jesus Christ. He will separate himself from what he is doing wrong and begin seeking restoration.

Many times, a Fallen Christian realizes his usefulness is empty and his life is going nowhere. His desire to do something positive, to find fulfillment in life, may encourage him to be restored.

These are great motivators. If the Restorer can build these motivations in the life of the Fallen Christian he is seeking to help, he will go a long way in helping to restore his friend or loved one.

> ***Psalms 42:1*** *– As the hart panteth after the water brooks, so panteth my soul after thee, O God.*

This verse illustrates powerful, positive motivators. If a Fallen Christian can become hungry for God, thirsty for the presence of Jesus Christ, they will want to return with all haste.

Thankfulness and Gratitude

This too can be a powerful motivator. Let me illustrate. Imagine crossing a street while I watch from the sidewalk. Suddenly, a car zips around a corner and bears down on you at a hundred miles an hour. I mutter to myself, "That car is going to run him over!" But I do nothing. I say nothing. I just stand there. Then, out of the corner of your eye, you see that car coming and you fling yourself out of the way, saving yourself by inches. How are you going to feel about me standing there on the sidewalk doing nothing?

You'll probably walk over, punch me, and yell, "Thanks a lot buddy! You could have said something! Done something! You almost let me die!" You have no desire, no will, to think good of me or to do me good.

If, however, I run out and shove you out of the way of that speeding car and get hit in your stead, your reaction will then be completely different. You will call 911. You will do everything you can to keep me alive. You will probably come visit me in the hospital. You may do other nice things for me. Why? So that I will save your life? No, you do these things out of a sense of gratitude, because I already saved your life.

Gratitude and thankfulness are powerful motivators.

> ***Colossians 1:12*** *– Giving thanks unto the Father, which hath made us meet to be partakers of the inheritance of the saints in light:*

God has done so many things for us. If the Restorer can help the Fallen Christian see what God has done for him, gratitude may be enough of a motivator to help restore him to Jesus Christ!

The Maniac of Gadara found a strong desire to serve God. Why? Because of gratitude for what Jesus did to deliver him from his bonds!

> ***Mark 5:18–19*** *– And when he was come into the ship, he that had been possessed with the devil prayed him that he might be with him. Howbeit Jesus suffered him not, but saith unto him, Go home to thy friends, and tell them how great things the Lord hath done for thee, and hath had compassion on thee.*

There is no doubt that this man had a tremendous motivation. The Restorer ought to help the Fallen Christian see how good God has been to him. If a sense of gratitude results, you have a positive motivator to help restore such a one!

Conclusion on Motivations

The Restorer must determine the motivations of the Christian he is trying to restore. There has to be some reason for him to come back. You, as the Restorer, may become his motivation. You may become his lifeline, his anchor. If so, you need to transfer that to Jesus Christ.

It is important to ensure that a walk with God becomes the foundation of a returning Christian's life. Without this relationship, his best attempts will only go so far.

16

Influencing the Heart

Read the story of Solomon and Rehoboam found in 1 Kings 12 as the basis for this chapter. The book of Proverbs is truly fascinating to any student of the Bible. It is primarily written by a father to a son. Solomon wrote the book in an effort to influence his son to maintain a walk with God and to gain knowledge, understanding, and wisdom. Solomon didn't want his son to ruin his life. Solomon didn't want his son to do something incredibly stupid.

But he failed.

Rehoboam, Solomon's son, rejected his father's counsel and destroyed the kingdom. His actions caused Israel to be split into two nations: the northern one became known as Israel and the southern one, as Judah. Somehow, somewhere, Solomon lost the ability to influence his son—all that wisdom and yet he failed. Why? What happened?

Why Solomon Lost His Influence Over His Son

I'm not going to pretend to be wiser than Solomon. I don't have to. Solomon explains why he lost his influence over his own son himself.

Proverbs 23:26 *– My son, give me thine heart, and let thine eyes observe my ways.*

Solomon teaches us in this verse exactly what it will take to properly influence his son.

1. Capturing his heart.
2. Being the right example to follow.

Solomon failed because he failed to win the heart of his son. Worse, he failed to be the right example for his son to follow. He wanted his son to follow his righteous ways, but Solomon turned from God and his words and actions no longer matched. He forsook everything he once held dear to him for his love of many different women (1 Kings 11:3). Instead of Solomon's words, his son followed his father's actions. Rehoboam did follow in his father's footsteps in the area of many wives, to his own destruction (2 Chronicles 11:21, 23).

It is hard to win someone's heart when you tell them to do one thing and then turn right around and do another. Solomon did not follow his own wisdom. We are all guilty of that. Possessing wisdom does not mean we have the character to follow it. Solomon apparently did not, and his son followed his ways rather than his wise advice.

Our ability to influence those around us is largely due to the consistency of our actions matching the words we say. Words have tremendous power and are most likely the single greatest human force in existence. Not even atomic weapons have done as much damage as words. But when our actions do not line up with our words, the words take on a negative influence. Interestingly, it is often the words we say that are held against us, more than our actions.

Solomon's influence was lost. His very powerful and wise words took on different meanings to a young Rehoboam—wrong ones.

How to Win Someone's Heart

Without the heart, your influence will do no good. Even the good things you do and say will be looked upon with suspicion and rejection. Unless you can win the heart of the Fallen Christian, you will not have any real influence.

Step 1: You Must Be the Right Example in Word and Deed

We've talked about it some, but let me emphasize it even more. Your actions need to match your words. Your life needs to be an example of your advice, a living illustration of why a Fallen Christian should heed your words. You don't have to be old and wise in order to have influence. You just need to be practicing what you preach.

A couple came to my office for marital counseling. They had been seeing a counselor already, but without any noticeable results. I asked, "This other guy, was he married?" The couple looked at each other and the wife replied, "No, I think he was divorced." That should tell you something, shouldn't it? Let your actions reflect your words. Your words are so powerful.

Step 2: You Must Believe in Him

When a Christian falls, makes a mistake, sins, or has destroyed something good, his greatest fear when trying to come back is that no one believes in him. He fears to come back to the gossip, the sad shakes of the head, the judgmental looks, and possible rejection. Left like this, he soon won't even want to come back. He'll turn his philosophy, his likes and dislikes, even his relationships over for something else, something that believes in him.

You may find this step hard. But it is necessary. Imagine a child who gets bad grades and only hears, "I knew you were good for nothing!" What motivation does he have to get good grades? None. But if someone believes in him and says, "I know you don't think you can do this, but I do. I believe in you. You can do this. Let me help." That may motivate him to earn good grades.

This is so true with even the most self-reliant person. Everyone needs someone to believe in him. Jesus believed in Peter. "Feed my sheep," He told Peter. Wow, someone thinks Peter is capable, that he is able! Guess what? He fed the sheep! Once Peter knew that Jesus still believed in him, knew that his failure had not closed every door, Peter was restored. Your loved one or friend can be restored too if the Restorer will find it within himself to believe in the fallen.

It may be more difficult than you think, however. Belief in someone implies trust. When you don't believe in someone, you don't trust him. If you do, then there is an element of trust. Oh Restorer, please understand the important role you play! When you make the attempt to restore someone, you also open yourself up to being hurt by the Fallen Christian. Know this in advance. Know also that the danger of betrayal is worth the risk if there is any hope of restoring the Fallen Christian.

Occasionally, I've said something like this to a Fallen Christian: "Listen, I believe in you. But do you know what that means? It means you have the power to hurt me. I'm trusting my heart to you, because I think you're worth it. But you can hurt me very deeply. Consider what you do, for you take me with you."

Risking betrayal and emotional pain is worth the price. You just need to be aware of the cost before you jump in. Trusting someone who has shattered all trust is a hard thing to do. Others may wonder at you, even think you are the fool. But every life salvaged, every life restored, every life brought back to the loving fellowship of Jesus Christ is worth the cost!

Believe in him! Go out on a limb. Be wise, however. I may not trust a thief with all my money, but I will endeavor to trust him with what I may afford to lose. I may approach the thief and say, "Look, you stole, and no one trusts you anymore. But I believe you want to be different. I believe you don't want this reputation. So let's prove everyone wrong. Here's $50 and a list of groceries. You can steal the money or you can show everyone that you can be trusted."

It's amazing how people like to build on something positive. This thief will keep my trust. He will like the feeling that comes with being thought trustworthy. He'll also love the increased fellowship. He won't want to destroy that. He will want to build on that. So many people are just looking for even one person to believe in them again. It may make all the difference in the world.

Step 3: Make Him Part of Your Life

In many ways, winning the heart of a Fallen Christian is much like winning the heart of your own children. Your children's hearts are won by making them a part of your life. Excluding them, isolating them, setting them aside, or only dealing with them from afar is not going to endear you to your children. Nor is it going to win you the heart of the Fallen Christian.

I remember my dad taking me and my brother as kids to his work after hours to play computer games. He worked in a large computer software development firm back in the early 1980s. This was before everyone in the world had personal computers. To my young eyes, everything was so cool! Hundreds of computer screens glowed like partially exposed treasure. My dad would allow me to play a game or two while he finished up some work, and then he would teach me some rudiments of computer programming. I felt special. I felt big. I felt part of my dad's life.

Notice what Jesus said and did to further endear his disciples to Him:

John 15:15 — Henceforth I call you not servants; for the servant knoweth not what his lord doeth: but I have called you friends; for all things that I have heard of my Father I have made known unto you.

Imagine how special those words made them feel! What a wonderful way to win someone's heart. What a wonderful way to influence them! And it worked! Not because it was pretense, but because Jesus meant it! Do you realize that the longest prayer recorded of Jesus praying was one that was specifically given for His disciples? Oh yes! No wonder Jesus had influence!

Invite the Fallen Christian to your home. Involve him in one of your projects. Ask his advice on something you intend to do. There are many ways to involve him. Doing so will help win his heart. Once you have his heart, you can influence him.

Step 4: Compliment and Praise Him

Very little in life endears you to someone as quickly as meaningful praise does.

> ***Proverbs 12:25*** *– Heaviness in the heart of man maketh it stoop: but a good word maketh it glad.*
>
> ***Proverbs 15:23*** *– A man hath joy by the answer of his mouth: and a word spoken in due season, how good is it!*
>
> ***Proverbs 25:11*** *– A word fitly spoken is like apples of gold in pictures of silver.*

I think we often miscalculate the value of a kind word. Let me give an example. Around our church—any church—there are many meaningful and purposeful jobs. Some of them, however, are rather thankless, such as cleaning the bathrooms. This is a necessary and vital job to the overall working of the church. But no one notices when it is done. They only notice when it is not done. For those who do it, having someone note the job well done goes a long way to motivating them to continue the job.

I urge parents to make sure they are praising their children at least as much as they get on their case for messing up. I've seen families where a child comes home with five A's and one F, and the parents launch into a rampage against the one F, while the five A's are not even mentioned. Do I think the child needs help in the area he got an F? Yes, I do. But the praise should be just as great, or greater, for the five A's!

I caution a wife not to be overly critical of her husband when his efforts to change fall way short of her expectations. Not hearing any encouraging words from her will only discourage him. He may just quit altogether and stop trying.

The same is true for a Fallen Christian. Most of us are hurt when all our good deeds are ignored and our failures are emphasized. A Fallen Christian needs to know that he can still be of value, that his life is important and meaningful. But he must hear it from you. One of my faults as a pastor is that I often fail to compliment people when they need it. I get so caught up in my own duties, jobs, and life that occasionally I fail to compliment someone who needs it.

Often, a single positive word or acknowledgement is all someone needs to keep going, to keep trying. Learn to look past the failures of the Fallen Christian and look for the positive things you can compliment. Sincerity and positivism go a long way toward capturing the heart of a Fallen Christian. This brings influence!

I think back on the teenagers whose hearts I succeeded in capturing. I had more influence over their lives than their own parents. In many cases, I gained this influence by merely praising them here and there. Often, the result never showed in their faces or actions, but by the trust they gave me. This gave me influence.

> ***Proverbs 27:2*** *– Let another man praise thee, and not thine own mouth; a stranger, and not thine own lips.*

Praising ourselves does no good. But here, being the other man is important. Hearing that someone else thinks well of him will help bring back the Fallen Christian.

17

Becoming More Influential

For this chapter, the story of Jehoshaphat and Ahab found in 1 Kings 22 and 2 Chronicles 18 will help teach us about influence and being an influence. In most relationships, there always seems to be one who has more influence over it than the other does. In the pursuit of helping to restore a Fallen Christian, we want the Restorer to have more influence than the Fallen Christian. It is very rare to find a relationship where there isn't someone in the relationship who tends to have more influence over it than the other one.

We can all think of marriages where the husband is more influential and marriages where the wife is more influential. Why is this? It is interesting that, as parents, we are more worried about the influence of other children on our own kids than we are excited about the influence our child has over another. We can fear the influence of other children, or we teach our children to be a positive influence on the other children.

This paradox really struck me as a student in Bible college. We were required to attend chapel every day, and I vividly recall two different preachers and their wildly different, but both equally valid, points. One warned us by saying, "Never hang around people who are less spiritual than you are, for everything descends to the lowest common denominator." Good advice, I thought.

But a few weeks later, a different preacher said this: "Try to hang around those less spiritual than you so that you can encourage them to rise to your level." This made sense too. But they both can't be right—can they?

We all know examples that make the statements of both preachers truisms. I warn young Christians all the time about falling back with their old friends. At first, they are adamant that their goals in hanging out with these old friends are purely noble. They have every intention of winning their friends to Christ and bringing them to church—so many of these end up dropping off the face of the planet as far as church is concerned. In other cases, I have witnessed faithful teenagers or adults influencing their families to start coming to church.

Nevertheless, there is a paradox. To obey the one preacher's admonition is to disobey the other one.

I think the key to reconciling the two and to gaining the right influence over those around us—particularly in the lives of the Fallen Christians—can be found in this story of Jehoshaphat.

Background Story

The nation of Israel, in the days of Rehoboam, was split into two kingdoms, north and south, Israel and Judah. Each had its own kings. In the north, the best king Israel ever had was a fellow by the name of Jehu. But the worst king was by far a villain named Ahab. Ahab took the daughter of the king of the Zidonians to wife, a wicked woman by the name of Jezebel.

There has rarely ever been such a wicked combination in the Bible. On a whim, Jezebel killed Naboth, a husbandman of a vineyard, simply because, I believe, Naboth's refusal to give his vineyard to her husband had sent Ahab into a royal pout. Disgusted at her husband and blaming Naboth for embarrassing the king—and her by extension—she had him murdered. It was from this woman Elijah fled, and it was this pair who tried to systematically destroy any God-fearing individual in the land. It was their daughter who murdered her own grandchildren in a bid to become queen of Judah. Guess where she learned her viciousness?

In contrast, Judah, the southern kingdom, had a few good kings. Joash (partly), Asa (partly) Hezekiah, Josiah, and one of the best ones was Jehoshaphat. For the most part, Jehoshaphat was a good king who did right in the eyes of the Lord. He never worshiped idols or built high places. He was a good king. He did only one thing wrong.

Jehoshaphat went up to visit Ahab. It's hard to imagine a simple visit to another king or head of state could be so disastrous for Jehoshaphat's own family. But it turned out to be the greatest and most destructive mistake he ever made—one that affected his son, his grandchildren, and his great-grandchildren profoundly.

*2 **Chronicles** 18:1 – Now Jehoshaphat had riches and honour in abundance, and joined affinity with Ahab.*

The word "affinity" means they cemented a treaty through a lawful marriage. On that fateful visit, Jehoshaphat's son, Jehoram, met Ahab's daughter. Something connected and the two were married. Unfortunately, she had a great deal more influence on him than he did on her.

*2 **Kings** 8:16–18 – And in the fifth year of Joram the son of Ahab king of Israel, Jehoshaphat being then king of Judah, Jehoram the son of Jehoshaphat king of Judah began to reign. Thirty and two years old was he when he began to reign; and he reigned eight years in Jerusalem. And he walked in the way of the kings of Israel, as did the house of Ahab: for the daughter of Ahab was his wife: and he did evil in the sight of the LORD.*

Jehoram didn't follow his daddy's footsteps. Instead, he followed his father-in-law's footsteps because his wife had more influence on him than he did on her. But why? It began when Jehoshaphat went into Ahab's sphere of influence. Ahab controlled the environment in Samaria. Ahab controlled the laws in Israel. Ahab and Jezebel controlled the food, the music, the dress—everything. They flaunted God's law and enforced only their own. It was to this environment that Jehoshaphat exposed his impressionable son. And it influenced him wrongly.

This is an essential key to understanding what happened. By entering the wrong environment, Jehoram's heart was captured by Jezebel's daughter. This is the danger of walking into a place where you are not in control of what goes on around you. You are the one being influenced.

Whoever Controls the Environment Does the Influencing

Notice the following verse:

> *2 Chronicles 18:2 – And after certain years he went down to Ahab to Samaria. And Ahab killed sheep and oxen for him in abundance, and for the people that he had with him, and persuaded him to go up with him to Ramothgilead.*

Who persuaded whom here? If you read the story, Jehoshaphat didn't want to go with Ahab but was unable to bring any real influence because he didn't control the environment. It was Ahab who provided the prophets and imprisoned the only true prophet among them. In Jehoshaphat's kingdom it would most certainly have gone differently.

> *2 Chronicles 18:4–5 – And Jehoshaphat said unto the king of Israel, Enquire, I pray thee, at the word of the LORD to day. Therefore the king of Israel gathered together of prophets four hundred men, and said unto them, Shall we*

> *go to Ramothgilead to battle, or shall I forbear? And they said, Go up; for God will deliver it into the king's hand.*

In this same visit, guess who met whom? From all appearances, the marriage was a whirlwind affair. It may be that Ahab and his wife pushed this hard in order to get Jehoshaphat to relent and go with them to Ramothgilead. Again, since it was Ahab's world, it was Ahab who had the ability to bring the greatest amount of pressure and influence to bear.

Later, when Jehoram married Ahab's daughter, she continued to control the environment even when she went back with him to Judah. It was this woman, Athaliah, who helped outlaw the Lord's priests, brought in the worship of false gods, and eventually murdered all her grandchildren, (except one) so she could be undisputed ruler in Judah. Some woman.

It all begins with who controls the environment. Even later, when the people rose up against Athaliah, Jehoiada the priest went out of his way to first control the environment before making a move against her (2 Chronicles 23:1–5).

Control and Influence

Whoever commands the surroundings will always feel the most in control. This is why, even in sports, the home court advantage is a tangible and noticeable thing. This is why teachers are often given leeway to setup their classrooms in a way that is most conducive to learning a particular subject.

When I pastored, I felt the most comfortable behind my own pulpit where I control the order of service. Being a guest speaker in someone else's pulpit is much harder. The host pastor still controls the environment; I am a guest in his house.

Attempting to influence someone who is in control of your surroundings is difficult. He will feel in control and will have instinctual desires to use it. Let me give you an example. We often go soul-winning in our church where we knock on other people's doors to share the Gospel with them. It is interesting to note that the same person who doesn't want to talk to you at their doorstep would be willing to talk to you if you happened to cross paths with them on the sidewalk in a park.

You see, when you go to their house, you are invading their domain. They are emboldened by the fact that they know they can control and even dictate what happens. But when you meet the same person walking in the park, they are often easier to influence. They are on public property. They know you have as much a right to be there as they do. It changes their attitude and even their willingness. It is often easier to influence someone when they are not in control of the surroundings.

This is one reason I find it incredibly important to counsel people in my office more so than in their own houses.

Authority and Influence

When you are in control of your surroundings, people will naturally defer to you and your decisions. For example, whoever owns the basketball gets to call the game. Others can leave, but if the owner takes his ball and goes home—game over.

I remember a ride home from work with a fellow Bible college student long ago. Everything began okay, but within a few minutes he reached over and turned on his radio. The music that came forth not only offended my ears but was also a violation of college policy regarding music. So I asked him to turn it off. He gave me an incredulous look and said, "My car. My rules. My music. You don't like that, you can get out."

I guarantee he would never have reacted in such a manner if I owned the car. But since he controlled the environment, he felt he had the authority to dictate the shots—even to the extent of its impact over his passenger. In this case, any argument I made, any reasoning I put forth, any logic I could suggest all would have been blatantly ignored. There was no way I could influence him under those circumstances.

With this in mind, understand that if you can control the environment, you can often dictate the shots and its impact on those you are trying to influence. This is essential. When I counsel in my office, I often ask for things—even demand things—of those I am trying to help. In my environment, my surroundings, they are much more apt to listen and agree to my terms.

Taped to the door of one of my neighbor's doors was a sign that read: "Take off your shoes before walking on the carpet. If you can't follow these basic rules, go back to wherever you came from." Again, his house, his rules. It all comes down to your perception of who controls the environment.

Control the Atmosphere If You Can't Control the Environment

Sometimes you can't control what is around you, how it looks, how it feels, or how it comes across. In such cases, try to control the tone and the mood. It is true: the environment contributes to the mood or tone of the atmosphere—just watch the opening introductions to a basketball game. But it is also true that if the visiting team is crushing the home team, the mood sours and the atmosphere is significantly changed from that of the beginning of the game.

The workplace, your school, even someone else's house are places where you normally have no control over the environment. Therefore, control the atmosphere. If you want to influence those around you, particularly a Fallen Christian, in an environment you cannot control, it is important that you try to take charge of the atmosphere. The atmosphere is formed from the attitudes of those involved, the language, the jokes, and the subjects of conversation. It's important to have some sort of control over these if you wish to have any influence.

Granted, it is always easier to control the atmosphere if you can also control the environment. Without the latter it is much more difficult to do the former.

I worked for a time at an auto parts manufacturing plant. I had absolutely no control over the environment. But I did set a tone around me. I brought a Bible to work, one I read on breaks. I made no attempt at hiding my faith at all. That set a mood or a tone that often dictated how others interacted with me. It is true that I was teased some, but in general, I had more influence over them than they did over me. I even started a cussing jar once and used the proceeds to help out a youth group. It was amazing how much the profanity dropped around me. In controlling the atmosphere, I became the unofficial pastor of my shift. People came to me for advice on marriage, childrearing, spiritual issues, and more.

Be warned, however: there are some environments where the only way to control the atmosphere is to do something drastic. At a party, for example, you will not be able to change the atmosphere unless you call the police. Doing something drastic rarely succeeds in gaining you influence. More often than not, people just resent it.

Taking control of the atmosphere must be done subtly. If you can't do it right, just get out.

Daniel (Daniel 1) was able to change the atmosphere in a hostile environment. He didn't do it obstinately, nor did he do it in open rebellion. He took control in a manner that resembled more of a diplomatic coup than anything else.

Here is a list of things to keep in mind when you are trying to control the atmosphere:

1. *Subjects of conversation* – If you can control the topics, you can set the tone.

2. *Jokes* – Humor, good or bad, often sets the mood or tone of an atmosphere.

3. *Language* – Especially profanity. Profanity in language often strips inhibitions to action. People who work themselves up to a fight don't use nice words. They use language that strips away their common sense and inhibitions.

4. *Music* – Studies show that music is a powerful mood setter. Again, pay attention to the type of music people who are spoiling for a fight listen to. People preparing to rob a store will not listen to "Jesus Loves Me."

The Restorer will have a hard time influencing the Fallen Christian unless he can adequately control the environment and atmosphere. Do this, and the opportunities to be a good and godly influence on behalf of the fallen is immeasurably greater.

Camps, for example, are very successful in changing the lives of teenagers. But then the camp controls the environment and atmosphere. Try reaching the same teenager's heart when he's surrounded by his friends at the public school. The Restorer must learn to be the right influence, but without the right environment or atmosphere, it makes your job that much more difficult.

18

Influencing the Influential

Study the story of Joseph found in Genesis 41 to understand this chapter better. Joseph, at the time of the story in Genesis 41, had lost most of the influence he ever had. He was sitting in jail, having succeeded in gaining the jailor's confidence and trust, but still a prisoner with little or no hope of release. Even after he succeeded in accurately interpreting the dreams of two fellow prisoners, he remained in prison for two more years before Pharaoh's dream and the lack of anyone to explain it finally brought him out of prison.

Joseph then went from a man of little influence to a man who could influence the most powerful man in the known world at the time. He was placed second in command and charged with saving Egypt in the coming famine. His influence with Pharaoh was so strong that Joseph was able to save his family from starvation, provide them with property from the best of the land, and continue in his seat of power until his death.

Harking back to his teenage years and a couple of dreams he once had, his own family, elder brothers and father, eventually bowed down to him and embraced his influence. Joseph became uniquely placed to influence the influential.

Why Joseph Gained So Much Influence

In this matter of restoring a Fallen Christian, what happens if the person who falls is someone you looked up to? What if the one who backslides is a pastor, parent, Sunday School teacher, or even your boss at work? Often, throughout this book, I have tried to make it clear that the Restorer must be in the right position to help restore a fellow Christian. True as that may be, there will be times when there is no one else to do it. So how do you influence the influential, the powerful, and the supposedly wiser person who has fallen?

The key is found in Genesis 41:37–40.

Genesis 41:37–40 — And the thing was good in the eyes of Pharaoh, and in the eyes of all his servants. And Pharaoh said unto his servants, Can we find such a one as this is, a man in whom the Spirit of God is? And Pharaoh said unto Joseph, Forasmuch as God hath shewed thee all this, there is none so discreet and wise as thou art: Thou shalt be over my house, and according unto thy word shall all my people be ruled: only in the throne will I be greater than thou.

We see a powerful man impressed with the wisdom and discreetness of a man who before this interview was nothing more than a forgotten prisoner. We see a king who recognizes the Spirit of God in someone else. And that is what always makes the difference.

You must be able to demonstrate to those more influential, more powerful, who have a stronger position, that you have the Spirit of God guiding your actions and decisions. Joseph never claimed he himself was smart or wise:

Genesis 41:16 — And Joseph answered Pharaoh, saying, It is not in me: God shall give Pharaoh an answer of peace.

Joseph's wisdom came from the Spirit of God. This is something he not only didn't hide, but something that became very obvious to Pharaoh. Joseph's relationship with God is what gave him the influence over people with whom he should normally not have had such an influence.

How the Restorer Can Gain This Influence

There may be times when you need this level of influence. You may be a teenager trying to bring back a wayward parent or a church member who wishes to salvage the ministry of his pastor, assistant pastor, or youth pastor. You may be a concerned employee seeking to divert your employer from a disastrous decision. You could be a wife desiring to restore your husband back to the spiritual leadership of your home. You may be a friend trying to restore a friend who once held a position of power and influence.

Step 1: You Must Have a Good Relationship with God

Christianity is about a relationship with God and Jesus Christ. If you take the relationship out of the religion, the religion is empty and vain. A marriage dies, not when the divorce papers are signed, but when the relationship ceases to be important to the couple.

If you ever want to have influence over the influential, you must work on your personal relationship with God!

> ***Romans 14:18***– *For he that in these things serveth Christ is acceptable to God, and approved of men.*
>
> ***Proverbs 3:3-5*** – *Let not mercy and truth forsake thee: bind them about thy neck; write them upon the table of thine heart: So shalt thou find favour and good understanding in the sight of God and man. Trust in the LORD with all thine heart; and lean not unto thine own understanding. In all thy ways acknowledge him, and he shall direct thy paths.*

Another example is, of course, Jesus Christ, who at a very young age increased in wisdom and stature and gained favor—the

Biblical word that indicates influence—with both God and man (Luke 2:52). Jesus, of course, had an incredible relationship with God the Father.

Take Daniel, who refused to defile himself because of his love for his God. The result was influence, first over the chief of the eunuchs and eventually over King Nebuchadnezzar. Daniel prayed three times a day and sought God in all things. No wonder he gained influence over the influential!

You must realize that people need to see something in you that will become greater than what you yourself could ever possess. They need to see in you wisdom beyond your years and discreetness that transcends your youth or lack of position. They need to see a God backing up your words and empowering your influence.

Step 2: You Must Be Humble

In influencing the influential, it is always necessary to exhibit a humbleness that disarms those whom you seek to influence. If you come across as harsh, demanding, or arrogant, you will fail to win them to your cause. Teenagers often fail to influence their parents' erroneous decisions because they come across as childish and throwing a tantrum. Church members often fail to be a help to their pastor when they come across too strongly, suggesting by their tone or body language that the pastor is a fool and an idiot. Employees fail to win over their boss when they make demands and begin to sow discord in the company.

Joseph never came across as arrogant. He came across as very humble.

Genesis 41:16 *– And Joseph answered Pharaoh, saying, It is not in me: God shall give Pharaoh an answer of peace.*

"It is not in me"—very good, Joseph! His refusal to take credit for any wisdom he possessed intrigued Pharaoh. Here was a man not seeking to cozy up to the most powerful ruler in the world. Here was a man who, quite simply and very honestly, just pointed to his God.

Humility is a quality that God looks at when determining your influence among men.

1 Peter 5:6 — Humble yourselves therefore under the mighty hand of God, that he may exalt you in due time:

Matthew 23:12 — And whosoever shall exalt himself shall be abased; and he that shall humble himself shall be exalted.

When you seek to influence the influential, approach them with humility. Daniel did, and look where it got him (Daniel 1). Joseph did, and we know where it got him!

Step 3: You Must Yield Yourself to the Spirit of God

Pharaoh recognized wisdom beyond the years and experience of Joseph. In fact, for that era, Joseph was still a very young man of only 30 years of age (Genesis 41:46). His only experience was running a household and helping in a jail. Not having ever gone to college or received a higher education, the wisdom of God shone through him.

This, more than anything else, is what will influence the influential in your life. Not you, but the wisdom you gained through your obedience to the Spirit of God.

1 Corinthians 12:7–8 — But the manifestation of the Spirit is given to every man to profit withal. For to one is given by the Spirit the word of wisdom; to another the word of knowledge by the same Spirit;

In the list of the gifts of the spirit here in 1 Corinthians 12, we see that the very first one is wisdom, followed immediately by knowledge. Of all the gifts, the gift to influence those around you is perhaps the greatest. Wisdom and knowledge are essential to that influence.

It is through the Spirit of God that we gain this level of influence. So, how does one yield himself to the Holy Spirit?

1. Walk in the Spirit by keeping the things of God in the forefront of your mind all day long (Romans 8:1–17).

2. Be filled with the Spirit by singing songs, hymns, and making melody in your heart to the Lord (Ephesians 5:18–19).

3. Continue to be filled with the Spirit by adopting a spirit of thanksgiving all the time (Ephesians 5:20).

4. Continue to be filled with the Spirit by humbling and submitting yourself to those around you (Ephesians 5:21).

If you can do these four things on a consistent basis, you will find yourself yielded to the Holy Spirit of God. Therefore, when you need to have influence over the influential in your life, to help restore a fellow Christian, God will grant you the favor and influence to do so.

The Restorer cannot be effective—cannot have any meaningful level of influence—without the Spirit of God. Don't be wise in your own eyes! Don't lean to your own understanding! Be sure to believe "it is not in me but in God…"

Step 4: Be a Good Listener and Ask Good Questions

Unless you have walked in the shoes of the one who fell, you will come across as condescending when you try to explain what he did wrong or how he could have done it better. This happened to Job. His friends had never gone through what he went through, and when they stopped listening and started talking, they lost all influence with Job.

Job 13:4 *– But ye are forgers of lies, ye are all physicians of no value.*

> ***Job 16:2*** *– I have heard many such things: miserable comforters are ye all.*

For seven days, his friends just sat with him while he grieved in silence. When Job finally opened his mouth and began talking, they felt obligated to challenge him. This robbed them of any influence they might have gained.

Let me see if I can explain this. A teenager has not the life experience to walk up to his parents and explain to them what they are doing wrong or how they should be doing it. Even if he is right, he has never raised a child, never paid the bills, never taken care of the insurance, never had a family to be responsible for, and never had to worry about a mortgage. Why would his parents listen to him? This teenager has no power of influence.

However, if he approaches his parents and asks good questions, listens to the responses, and asks more questions, the parents perceive a different attitude and spirit in their teenager. This will cause them to have more respect for the teenager, giving the teenager influence he never had before.

It is pointless to lecture a fallen leader on what he should or should not have done if you have never walked in his shoes. Be a good listener. Ask good questions. It is amazing how much influence a person who really listens has.

Part Two – Becoming Influential in the Life of the Fallen

PART THREE

Helping the Healing Process

Goals and Purpose of This Part of the Book

The Restorer will often be called upon to assist in the healing process of the Fallen Christian as he comes back. Success in bringing a backslidden or fallen Christian back to God is not complete until the fallen Christian has healed from the damage done to himself spiritually, emotionally, and mentally.

The Restorer needs to help the healing process.

James 5:16 *– Confess your faults one to another, and pray one for another, that ye may be healed. The effectual fervent prayer of a righteous man availeth much.*

The following chapters will concentrate on how the Restorer can assist in the healing process. Take heed to this section. One of the most prolific obstacles to restoration is unhealed emotional injuries. These emotional injuries can and will destroy any future a person has. Healing must take place.

Restoration is not complete until the Fallen Christian has healed.

All of the following chapters assume that the Restorer has won the Fallen Christian's heart. As discussed in previous chapters, you must have the heart of the one you are trying to help if you seek to have any influence in his life.

19

Removing Spiritual Infection

When a person violates their own conscience, dream, or moral compass, they inflict on themselves an emotional injury. A Christian who backslides or falls away will cause an emotional wound that is difficult to heal.

In order to come back completely, a Christian must heal from these emotional wounds.

The problem, however, is that emotional wounds of this nature become diseased with a type of spiritual infection. This infection prevents the wound from healing quickly or well and can poison a person's thinking and recovery. An infected wound will not heal. It may be ignored for a time, but when a situation or circumstances brush up against the wound, it will hurt and can reverse all the progress made in the restoration process.

The wound could be anything. It could be a troubled childhood, a bad relationship, a disappointment, or a tragedy. What makes a recovering alcoholic fall back into alcoholism? What makes a recovering drug addict return to the drugs? Often it is an emotional wound that has never healed. This wound often drives people right back into the sin or darkness they were trying to recover from.

The Restorer must become aware of these emotional injuries and seek to help them heal. The first step is to get rid of the spiritual infection that may be keeping the wound from healing in the first place.

Hebrews 12:14–17 *– Follow peace with all men, and holiness, without which no man shall see the Lord: Looking diligently lest any man fail of the grace of God; lest any root of bitterness springing up trouble you, and thereby many be defiled; Lest there be any fornicator, or profane person, as Esau, who for one morsel of meat sold his birthright. For ye know how that afterward, when he would have inherited the blessing, he was rejected: for he found no place of repentance, though he sought it carefully with tears.*

Esau (Genesis 25) sold his birthright for a bowl of soup. Later, when he realized what he had done, it became a wound infected with the spirit of bitterness. This bitterness resulted in much pain for him and his family. His failure developed bitterness. Bitterness led to rejection. Rejection led to murderous desires.

It is important to understand that for anyone to be restored, there must first be a realization of one's own failures. This is not easy. Who likes to be faced with his own weaknesses? Who likes to be confronted by his own evil and sin? For many, the recognition of these failures is traumatic. They don't deal with them appropriately and in most cases try to ignore them. This makes healing difficult and a relapse more likely.

A word, sound, sight, or smell could unearth all the pain, agony, bitterness, and fears that they thought were safely buried. The effect on the Christian is traumatic. Often, it drives him right back into the mire he is so desperately seeking to escape.

Cleansing the Emotional Wound with Truth

The healing process for all emotional injuries begins with the truth.

> *John 8:32 – And ye shall know the truth, and the truth shall make you free.*

For our purposes here, we will define truth as "exposing that which is hidden."

In essence, that is what all truth is. It is an attempt to bring into the light that which has lain hidden or covered. Deception, or a lie, is an attempt to hide, to bury, to cover up something. Truth, therefore, is a confession, a revealing of a pain or an injury that needs to be exposed in order to heal.

> *Proverbs 16:6 – By mercy and truth iniquity is purged: and by the fear of the LORD men depart from evil.*

After years of counseling, I've learned that emotional injuries must be exposed in order to begin the healing process. The guilt of a wrongdoing or even victim's guilt is always associated with emotional trauma and will never be purged, never be reconciled until it comes out into the light.

The common method of dealing with emotional trauma is to bury it, to hide it, to cover it up, and then to hopefully ignore it. But it can't be ignored. An infection—and that is what guilt is—can't be ignored. It will spread and damage so many other areas of your life. I've met many Christians who attempt to come back from a sin, addiction, or failure. Many of them tragically slip right back into the cesspool they were trying to escape due to an emotional wound that never healed.

> *1 John 1:9 – If we confess our sins, he is faithful and just to forgive us our sins, and to cleanse us from all unrighteousness.*

Notice that the cleansing of the wound cannot begin until the wound is first exposed—or confessed as the Scriptures put it. It is the act of revealing the wound to God, as our Great Physician, that allows Him to set about cleansing the wound from the infection, unrighteousness, or guilt.

This is a biblical model that is taught throughout the Scriptures. Observe the following verse:

> ***James 5:16*** *– Confess your faults one to another, and pray one for another, that ye may be healed. The effectual fervent prayer of a righteous man availeth much.*

The word "faults" here is a direct reference to our sins or transgressions. It is referring to the guilt that always accompanies the emotional wound. So many people carry the guilt of what they did or what happened to them around with them like an open wound. This guilt plays havoc with our emotional stability, causing irrational anger and allowing our fears to dominate our thinking and actions. A wife can fear men—including her husband—due to sexual molestation as a child. A husband can erupt into rage because of physical abuse as a teenager. Faults can cause a Restored Christian to fall once again.

This guilt must be purged for real restoration to take place. It begins with truth, the exposure of what happened, the revealing of what—in most cases—happened years and years ago.

In some manner, the Fallen must confront his guilt. He must get it out. He needs to address it, talk about it, pray about it, and face it. He must learn to forgive the wrongs done to him and to forgive himself for the wrongs he has done. He will fear this and seek to avoid this. For many, these wounds have been part of their lives for a long time. They have buried them long and deep. The Restorer must find a way to help lance the wound of the spiritual infection and give the Fallen a real chance to heal.

Let me see if I can illustrate this further. A boy falls off his bike and scrapes his arm up rather badly. He runs to Mom, but in so doing, he instinctively puts his hand over the wound and covers it up. The very first thing mom says is, "Let me see it." The boy needs to reveal the wound for inspection, reveal the injury so that it can be cleansed. But often, children don't want to do that. Revealing the wound seems to bring about more pain. But it is necessary in order for Mom to begin the healing process properly. Mom will then cleanse the wound—a process that may sting—in order to prevent infection from setting in. Once the wound is infected, it will not heal.

Emotional wounds are the same way. If you are the Restorer, you may need to ask to see the wound of the Fallen Christian you are trying to help. God lovingly explains that you must confess your sin before He can cleanse you of all unrighteousness. If we are to help the Fallen Christian heal, we need them to confess their faults—to confront the truth.

If you think about it, the things that bother you the most about your past are not the things you got caught for. It's the things you got away with and no one—no one but you—knows what you did. To this day you are still hiding those things. To this day they still affect you.

John 8:32 – And ye shall know the truth, and the truth shall make you free.

Taking the Fallen Christian's Confession

No one can truly forgive sins except Jesus Christ. The Bible, however, does command us to confess our faults—sins and transgressions—to another Christian so others can help us heal. In this respect, there are times when you need to allow another Christian to confess to you.

James 5:16 – Confess your faults one to another, and pray one for another, that ye may be healed. The effectual fervent prayer of a righteous man availeth much.

The process is one born of love, not judgment. Certainly, we must confess our sins to God. There is no doubt about that. But it is also true that confessing to our fellow Christians is an integral part of the healing process.

Here are the main benefits of confession:

1. It allows the Fallen Christian to expose a wound to be cleansed.
2. It allows the Fallen Christian to find forgiveness from fellow Christians.
3. It allows the Fallen Christian to find mercy from fellow Christians.
4. It allows the Fallen Christian to discover hope.

Forgiveness, mercy, and hope are essential to the healing process of any Fallen Christian. These are things the Restorer can provide. When a Fallen Christian can find these things from those around him, he can then begin to forgive himself.

If, however, he is condemned and ostracized, he will never heal and he will never come back. We lose many Christians because fellow Christians are more inclined to judge than to dispense mercy and hope.

As the Restorer, your reaction to a Fallen Christian's confession should be one of love. Prayer is a crucial part of the healing process as well. Pray for them. Allow them to hear you praying for them. Set time aside just to pray for them in their presence. Allow them to hear your voice filled with mercy and forgiveness. Allow them the chance to cleanse their wound. Allow them to seek forgiveness from God and allow God to cleanse them from all unrighteousness.

Some of the most productive Christians are those who have been restored. In fact, I would venture to say that many of your heroes of the faith are Restored Christians—including some of your favorite Bible characters.

It is not your place to justify a Fallen Christian's sin or failure. It is not your place to judge it. It is not your place to excuse it. It is not your place to lessen the consequences. It is your place to provide a path back to restoration.

20

The Reconciliation Process

I will go out on a limb here and state what I believe to be the overall theme of the Bible. I've heard many themes proposed, but the one that encompasses all of them and is the basis of every verse from Adam's sin until the end of Revelation is this: Reconciliation.

Reconciliation is the basis for every act of God since the Garden of Eden. It is the genius of the animal sacrifices, the priesthood, the temple, the Ark of the Covenant, the promises, Jesus' death on the cross, and the driving force of His love.

God would rather have reconciliation than punishment.

> ***Ezekiel 18:23*** – *Have I any pleasure at all that the wicked should die? saith the Lord GOD: and not that he should return from his ways, and live?*

To the Fallen Christian, God says, "Come back!" We, as Restorers, ought to have the same attitude. We ought to seek reconciliation rather than condemnation.

Lest this concept be taken out of context, let me add that God does judge, He does condemn. This is undeniable in Scripture. The

Bible is full of judgment on sin and there is condemnation of sin as well. As true as that may be, God would rather have reconciliation than condemn. In Christ, we have no more condemnation (Romans 8:1), but that doesn't mean God won't judge us (2 Corinthians 5:10).

This book isn't about what God does; it is about God's command to restore a Fallen Christian. In that context, we are to leave any judgment and condemnation up to God and seek reconciliation.

The three tools God uses to try to bring about reconciliation are these:

1. *Love* (A selfless act with no thought of reward)
2. *Grace* (God's provision for our utter insufficiencies)
3. *Forgiveness* (An act of mercy that drops all charges)

We will examine each of these tools to discover how they facilitate reconciliation. Our goal is to help restore the Fallen Christian by reconciling him to God. God has given us these tools to aid in that endeavor.

The Reconciliation Tool of Love

John 3:16–18 – For God so loved the world, that he gave his only begotten Son, that whosoever believeth in him should not perish, but have everlasting life. 17 For God sent not his Son into the world to condemn the world; but that the world through him might be saved. 18 He that believeth on him is not condemned: but he that believeth not is condemned already, because he hath not believed in the name of the only begotten Son of God.

Love is a selfless act or deed that is often sacrificial in nature. It is the laying down of something important—vital even—for the sake of another without the expectation of reward or recompense. This is often done by giving up something so that another can get something.

> *John 15:13* – *Greater love hath no man than this, that a man lay down his life for his friends.*

Love is not a mushy feeling. Love is a sacrificial act. It is a tool to reconcile differences. After all, God told us to love our enemies! So what exactly does love reconcile? Love is the tool that reconciles a difference of opinion, like or dislike, or need.

No two people on the planet will ever agree on everything. You won't share every like and every dislike. Love reconciles these differences. Love allows you to have a solid relationship despite these differences.

Jesus' death was an act of love. God cannot tolerate sin—either my sin or your sin. Yet His love found a way to reconcile us to him!

> *2 Corinthians 5:18* – *And all things are of God, who hath reconciled us to himself by Jesus Christ, and hath given to us the ministry of reconciliation;*

He is holy. We are unholy. He is just. How do we reconcile these differences? Through love.

In the same way, our love overcomes all differences. A Fallen Christian's sin and guilt can be dealt with by a hefty dose of love. When we love the Fallen Christian, we reconcile differences. These differences are often stark, obvious, and sometimes even odious. Yet love covers a multitude of sins.

> *Proverbs 10:12* – *Hatred stirreth up strifes: but love covereth all sins.*

This in no way implies that we are to ignore sin. Sin can't be ignored. Yet love has the unique property to bridge the gap created by sin and bring about reconciliation. Hatred, on the other hand, only increases the differences.

Love allows another person to have a different opinion. Love allows another to have different likes and dislikes. Love allows you to get along with those with whom you do not share much in common. This is how God gets along with us…sinners.

Use love to surmount your differences with the Fallen Christian. You will find, when you can perform an act of sacrificial love, that your differences no longer matter.

The Reconciliation Tool of Grace

Love reconciles differences of opinions, likes, dislikes, and even of purpose and motive. Grace, however, is a tool of reconciliation that reconciles something else.

> ***Ephesians 2:8–9*** *– For by grace are ye saved through faith; and that not of yourselves: it is the gift of God: 9 Not of works, lest any man should boast.*

Grace is the provision you give for someone else's insufficiency or weakness. In other words, an act of grace is where you provide your strength to help another overcome what they could not overcome on their own.

> ***Hebrews 4:16*** *– Let us therefore come boldly unto the throne of grace, that we may obtain mercy, and find grace to help in time of need.*

Grace, therefore, reconciles your strengths and weakness to another's strengths and weaknesses.

Grace is often thought of as unmerited favor. I don't totally disagree; I just think such a definition is too simplistic. God's grace is His provision for our insufficiencies.

> ***2 Corinthians 3:5*** *– Not that we are sufficient of ourselves to think any thing as of ourselves; but our sufficiency is of God;*

> ***2 Corinthians 9:8*** *— And God is able to make all grace abound toward you; that ye, always having all sufficiency in all things, may abound to every good work:*
>
> ***2 Corinthians 12:9*** *— And he said unto me, My grace is sufficient for thee: for my strength is made perfect in weakness. Most gladly therefore will I rather glory in my infirmities, that the power of Christ may rest upon me.*

Grace is a tool to reconcile our faults and weaknesses to a God who has no faults and who has no weaknesses. It is also a tool the Restorer can use to help reconcile the Fallen Christian back to the church and to the fellowship of the believers.

Put in its simplest form, grace is where you use your strength to help another's weaknesses.

This effort on the part of the Restorer goes a long way to help the Fallen Christian. Let me give an example. A family nearly fell apart due to financial trouble. Neither the husband nor the wife understood money or finances. They were in massive debt and it nearly destroyed their marriage. We stepped in and helped them develop a workable budget. We reduced their debt, even to the point of negotiating with some of the creditors. We managed their money and helped them through it. Once their finances began to improve, so did their marriage. This is grace.

If a Fallen Christian is struggling with an addiction, show some grace. Dig in and lend a hand. Use your strengths to help his weaknesses. As I mentioned back in Chapter One, I knew an alcoholic who drank nearly $10,000 worth of booze in roughly a two-month time frame. I went to the bar and literally pulled him out at his wife's request. Instead of condemning him, I met with him every morning for a Bible study. I literally replaced his character with my character until it became his own. He now pastors a church. This is grace.

The Restorer must learn to give grace to the Fallen Christian if he wants to help reconcile him. A person who is wounded or afraid needs someone to lend him strength until he can stand on his own.

The Reconciliation Tool of Forgiveness

Forgiveness is an act of mercy. It is dropping all charges accumulated due to the wrong. You cannot do this for everyone affected. You can only drop the charges that pertain to you. To be frank, I can't forgive a Fallen Christian a wrong inflicted against someone else. I can only forgive what was done to me.

Sin, however, usually affects everyone. Therefore, there is mercy you can grant to the Fallen Christian.

Love reconciles differences of ideology, opinion, purpose, and motive. Grace reconciles differences between strengths and weaknesses. Forgiveness reconciles differences caused by a wrong or an injury inflicted upon you.

Ephesians 1:3–7 *– Blessed be the God and Father of our Lord Jesus Christ, who hath blessed us with all spiritual blessings in heavenly places in Christ: According as he hath chosen us in him before the foundation of the world, that we should be holy and without blame before him in love: Having predestinated us unto the adoption of children by Jesus Christ to himself, according to the good pleasure of his will, To the praise of the glory of his grace, wherein he hath made us accepted in the beloved. In whom we have redemption through his blood, the forgiveness of sins, according to the riches of his grace;*

Love yields a strength, grace uses strength to balance a weakness, and forgiveness accepts a weakness. Forgiveness is essential to the reconciliation process. No two people can spend a lot of time together without eventually hurting each other in some way. It may be unintentional, but it still occurs. Forgiveness allows for the other person's weaknesses and mistakes that may have injured you in some way. Since we all have these weaknesses, forgiveness will allow reconciliation.

> ***2 Corinthians 2:6–11*** *– Sufficient to such a man is this punishment, which was inflicted of many. So that contrariwise ye ought rather to forgive him, and comfort him, lest perhaps such a one should be swallowed up with overmuch sorrow. Wherefore I beseech you that ye would confirm your love toward him. For to this end also did I write, that I might know the proof of you, whether ye be obedient in all things. To whom ye forgive any thing, I forgive also: for if I forgave any thing, to whom I forgave it, for your sakes forgave I it in the person of Christ; Lest Satan should get an advantage of us: for we are not ignorant of his devices.*

True reconciliation will take place once the Fallen Christian recognizes that other Christians are willing and able to forgive him. This provides hope. And hope is essential to faith.

Conclusion

In brief, let's review how the tools of reconciliation help in the restoration process of a Fallen Christian.

1. *Love* – Reconciles the differences between ideology, opinion, purpose, likes, dislikes, and motives.
2. *Grace* – Reconciles the differences between one's strengths and another's weaknesses.
3. *Forgiveness* – Reconciles the differences or hurts created due to a wrong or injurious sin.

With these three tools, the Restorer has a powerful arsenal at his disposal to help restore a Fallen Christian. Wielded properly, the Restorer can help reconcile a Fallen Christian back to the loving embrace of Jesus Christ.

21

Rebuilding Trust and Purpose

Trust is a fickle thing. It takes a tremendous amount of effort to earn it, yet very little to destroy it. Unfortunately, in most cases, a Fallen Christian has shattered everyone's trust in him. Rebuilding that trust is done neither quickly nor easily.

Trust is a key factor that every Fallen Christian seeking restoration looks for. It is a benchmark they use to determine if they can be accepted by their fellow Christians. Recovering addicts, for example, often struggle with the lack of trust shown by family and friends. They don't understand why people can't trust them easily. Many find this lack of trust frustrating and even damaging to their recovery. Yet, trust must be earned. And it is never easily earned.

But giving trust when it has not been earned is impossible. Ever heard someone say, "Trust me"? Begging trust, demanding trust, or even asking for trust implies there is a reason for mistrust. The Fallen Christian wants to be trusted once again. Yet it is not a simple thing to make them a Sunday School teacher after having destroyed the trust of the children and parents. It is never so easily regained.

The Restorer's job is not so much to trust the Fallen Christian as it is to provide a means by which the Fallen Christian can rebuild that trust.

In a similar manner, we see our purpose in life tied directly to the trust we are given. Our ability to influence and affect those around us in a positive manner is dependent upon the trust we have earned. Purpose, therefore, is a natural extension of that trust. Without the trust of those we interact with, our purpose is diminished or negated.

A Christian seeking to be restored needs purpose. He needs direction. Yet that purpose and direction is an avenue supplied by the trust of those around him—often something he has destroyed. The Restorer needs to supply the means by which he can earn both back.

Paul, before he got saved, spent a lot of time betraying Christians into the hands of their tormentors. After his conversion, he sought to join with those he once hunted.

> ***Acts 9:26*** *– And when Saul was come to Jerusalem, he assayed to join himself to the disciples: but they were all afraid of him, and believed not that he was a disciple.*

Paul, named Saul at the time, found his purpose voided because no one trusted him. It wasn't until Barnabas decided to take him under his wing and provide him with a means to earn trust that Paul finally found his purpose.

> ***Act 9:27*** *– But Barnabas took him, and brought him to the apostles, and declared unto them how he had seen the Lord in the way, and that he had spoken to him, and how he had preached boldly at Damascus in the name of Jesus.*

This is what a Restorer must do. We need more Christians to be like Barnabas.

Teaching the Fallen Christian How to Earn Your Trust

Proverbs 25:19 – Confidence in an unfaithful man in time of trouble is like a broken tooth, and a foot out of joint.

Luke 16:10 – He that is faithful in that which is least is faithful also in much: and he that is unjust in the least is unjust also in much.

It is much easier to lose someone's trust than it is to gain it. And few people are comfortable when someone says, "Trust me." Having to say it at all makes you wonder.

Love is something you give. It is a tool of reconciliation. Trust is something you earn, so if you have someone's trust, treat it like a rare coin. Don't spend a rare, $1,000 quarter on a 25-cent piece of gum. If you have someone's trust, it is a very special thing.

There are several factors that go into earning someone's trust. As a Restorer, you need to teach the one you are helping how to regain people's trust. The following four areas are the keys to earning trust back:

1. Having a trustworthy personal history.
2. The ability to meet other's expectations of behavior consistently.
3. The willingness to live within the rules of interaction set forth by the one from whom you are trying to earn trust.
4. The demonstration of effort in the eyes of those watching.

Actually, none of this sounds fair until you realize people who want your trust have to demonstrate the same things to you. Let's look at them one at a time and see how they can help a Fallen Christian seeking restoration rebuild trust.

Area 1: Personal History

This one needs almost no comment. Your record is a hard thing to live down. If you've messed up in the past, are now repentant, and wish to change, then study the other three factors in this chapter.

To the best of your ability, have a track record that demonstrates trust to people. Show people that you are trustworthy. If people know you are a gossip, they probably won't tell you any secrets. It's just the way it is.

Area 2: The Ability to Meet Expectations of Behavior

Everyone has expectations. Sometimes they are unrealistic and other times they simply don't make much sense. But people expect other people to react in certain manners and ways. If they don't get the expected result, it makes it hard to earn that person's trust.

If I walk up to someone with a friendly smile and reach out to shake his hand and he hits me in the face for it, I will find it impossible to trust him the next time I see him. His reaction was so far outside my expectations that I find I can't trust him.

I expect my neighbor to respect my property. If I come out one morning and find him spraying graffiti all over my garage door, I'll not trust him. I expect a store to give me the correct change. If they cheat me, I lose faith in them and won't go back. I expect a judge to be fair. If he is not, I lose respect and trust in his ability. I expect my friends to help me when I'm in trouble. Maybe I shouldn't, but most do, and when they refuse to help, I lose faith and trust.

I'm not saying that everyone's expectations are fair, balanced, or even justified. This is just the way it is. Everyone has expectations. If you fail to meet those expectations of behavior, then you will struggle to gain their trust.

As a Restorer, your job is to provide realistic expectations and make those expectations clear. It is difficult to earn someone's trust when the means to do so is hidden. Let him know what you expect. Spell it out. Explain to him that if he can keep to your expectations, he will begin to earn your trust.

There need to be clearly defined goals so the Fallen Christian has something to measure his progress by. If, however, he fails to abide by the expectations, you start over. You back up to Step One and try again. Trust is earned by taking responsibility for your responsibilities. Give him minor responsibilities and tell him that more responsibility will come depending on how he handles what is given.

Area 3: The Ability to Live Within the Rules of Interaction

Every relationship has rules. These rules, spoken or unspoken, govern the relationship. If you interact with someone outside of his acceptable rules of interaction, he will not trust you. This differs from the last point in that expectations are a foundation for responsibility, but relationship rules are a foundation for interaction.

Again, this doesn't sound very fair. But it is reality. Every relationship has rules. It is more than mere expectations of behavior, but specific guidelines of interaction. A marriage has certain rules; if those rules are broken, so is the trust. When we interact with people there are always written and unwritten rules.

My wife wears a wedding ring. That ring defines various rules of interaction with every man who is not her husband. If someone attempts to violate those rules, we have a very serious trust issue.

All parents have rules for their children. If the child wishes to earn his parent's trust, he needs to follow the rules. His willingness to follow these rules earns trust. When teenagers choose friends who are clearly outside the framework of the rules of interaction, they damage their parents' trust.

The Restorer needs to lay down some ground rules. These rules need to be clear. Don't expect a Fallen Christian to understand or be knowledgeable about rules you have not clearly defined. These rules of interaction give him a basis for earning your trust.

Area 4: The Demonstration of Effort

Emphasize how important their effort is to rebuilding trust. Explain that their effort will be measured and weighed by everyone around them. Trust isn't gifted. It is earned. Challenge the Fallen Christian to make a lot of effort to earn trust back.

But caution him about measuring his success by other people's reactions to his effort. People whose trust has been broken will be very reserved, very withdrawn. Help him to measure his success by the effort he is putting forth. Use effort as the benchmark, not other people's reactions.

Effort is the only thing a returning Christian can control. He can't control another person's actions. Set goals of effort and measure everything by the effort.

Helping the Fallen Christian to Find Purpose

As already explained, purpose is often born out of trust. It is hard to fulfill a purpose when we cannot engender the trust necessary to succeed at it. Still, purpose in life is essential. God did not create us to waste our lives. God created us to do something constructive with it.

I know of a man who, after coming out of a drug-addicted lifestyle, decided to take his experiences and help other addicts. Many pastors today were once purposeless and untrustworthy but changed their lives around and decided to use their experiences to help others. Many books are written for similar purposes. We applaud these people—and rightly so.

Help the one you are trying to restore to find some purpose. Encourage him to act upon what he can do. It may be as simple as mowing someone's yard or standing before other hurting people and talking about Jesus Christ. Purpose is needed.

Here are a few guidelines to use in helping someone find purpose:

1. Provide something that can be done now. Grand ideas can be exciting, but overwhelming when he doesn't yet have the trust or character necessary to accomplish it.

2. Give him assistance in fulfilling it. Don't abandon him. Give guidance, advice, and assistance.

3. Applaud his efforts. Point out how they are making a difference. Deflect praise from you to them.

4. Gradually increase responsibility as he becomes more comfortable and demonstrates faithfulness in his purpose.

5. Publicly choose him over others in areas that are nonessential. Eventually, after he has proven trustworthy, you can choose him for essential areas. Until then, he needs to feel trusted.

6. Surround him with people who are eager for him to succeed.

Every Christian is needed. Every Christian is important.

__1 Corinthians 12:18–23__ – But now hath God set the members every one of them in the body, as it hath pleased him. And if they were all one member, where were the body? But now are they many members, yet but one body. And the eye cannot say unto the hand, I have no need of thee: nor again the head to the feet, I have no need of you. Nay, much more those members of the body, which seem to be more feeble, are necessary: And those members of the body, which we think to be less honourable, upon these we bestow more abundant honour; and our uncomely parts have more abundant comeliness.

Purpose is essential to the makeup of any individual. If you tell a person, "We don't need you around here," you will fundamentally damage the restoration process. Purpose provides a sense of belonging, of having a place in the scheme of things. Rip that away or fail to give it, and the Christian seeking restoration may plunge back into the darkness you are trying to pull him from.

22

A Final Word to the Restorer

The key to a Fallen Christian's restoration is still the Restorer. In every case of a Fallen Christian described in this book, the Restorer plays a vital role in bringing him back. Even if the only thing you do is say, "Welcome back!" it could be enough.

No matter who the Fallen Christian may be—a friend, loved one, church member, or family member—he or she needs a Restorer. Your importance cannot be underestimated. Each type of Fallen Christian mentioned in this book describes, in some way, those you know who have fallen away from our Saviour. The tips and suggestions listed in this book are designed to help you help them.

Patience is required, however, and a merciful heart. But patience is a tool you use to assist in the restoration process. Notice the following verses:

> *James 1:3–4 – Knowing this, that the trying of your faith worketh patience. But let patience have her perfect work, that ye may be perfect and entire, wanting nothing.*

Permanent change rarely happens instantaneously. Art, for example, is accomplished through painstaking attention to detail and patient perseverance. Perfection is the result of patience.

Don't be discouraged when the one you are trying to help lets you down, betrays your trust, or slips back. Don't take his failure personally. Don't let it become your failure. You only fail when you quit. Remember, helping restore a Fallen Christian does as much good for your own faith as it does the one you are trying to help.

The cause of Christ is only furthered by your efforts to love and restore a Fallen Christian. These fallen individuals can become a powerful force for good if they are brought back.

Imagine how the Bible would have gone if Peter hadn't been restored. There might have been no Pentecost and, most likely, no church in Jerusalem. Jesus could have spent that time in winning another soul to Christ, but instead He took the time to restore a fallen believer instead. But by so doing, that once Fallen Christian, now restored, went out and won thousands and thousands to Christ.

God bless you and those you love.

23

Questions and Answers for the Restorer

Hopefully, these questions and answers will provide you with the bulk of the help that you could not find elsewhere in these pages. Look them over. I pray they will help you restore your friend or loved one.

Question: What do you do if a Fallen Christian exhibits traits from several of the different types of Fallen Christians you talk about in this book?

Answer: This is not an uncommon problem. Since every person is unique and different, it would be very rare to find a Fallen Christian who perfectly matches one of the various types listed in this book. The solutions given in this book are meant to guide you in dealing with certain characteristics and personalities. You may need to design a unique working model from the various solutions provided in this book specific to the individual you are trying to help.

For example, if someone has made a mistake such as Peter did, he could be depressed while attempting to justify the mistake like King Saul did. In such a case, you may need to take the procedures from both chapters to help restore this Fallen Christian.

Question: What do you do if the hindrance to a Fallen Christian's restoration is another Christian—not me—within the same church or the same family?

Answer: This occurs when two Christians have a falling out or one has been hurt by the Fallen Christian's sin. In order to help the Fallen Christian's restoration process, it will be necessary to deal with the one hindering the process. If this is impossible, then you may need to seek another place for the Fallen Christian to go and be accepted.

Discord among the brethren is something God hates (Proverbs 6:19). The Scriptures teach us that we must first seek to reconcile with our brethren before we can correctly work on ourselves (Matthew 5:23–24). In some cases, you will need to involve more people in an effort to reconcile the two. But until reconciliation can be achieved, they will not love each other as they should… as we are told we must (1 John 3:14–21).

Before you can make much progress, you need to achieve some sort of reconciliation between the two at odds. Otherwise, the Fallen Christian may feel the other's bitterness and resist the restoration process. The other one may feel hurt by the attention and love you are bestowing on someone who hurt him. This may facilitate even more bitterness.

From one point of view, you are dealing with two Fallen Christians, not one. The second one may fit under an Absalom or Cain type.

Question: What do I do if the Fallen Christian admits a crime to me? Am I protected if I keep it in confidence?

Answer: First, you will need to seek out the law enforcement agency in your area and ask them that question. You may need to consult with a lawyer. In general, petty crimes that have exceeded the statute of limitations can be kept in confidence—still check on the laws in your area to be certain. But major crimes will more than likely need to be reported. Either way, follow the advice of your local law enforcement agency or lawyer. Certain crimes, no matter what, need to be reported immediately. Murder or sexual crimes are among the ones you can't keep to yourself.

The very first thing I do, when a crime is admitted to me, is try to get them to turn themselves in. This is best all the way around. If they won't and you feel, due to your policy, you must be the one to turn them in, then do so.

Question: In restoring someone who has hurt or wronged another individual, does the restoration excuse the crime or the wrong? What about justice? What about the victim?

Answer: The restoration process is not an excuse or justification for a wrong. However, a Fallen Christian who is not being restored will have a hard time making restitution for any number of reasons. But one who is being restored is a lot more willing to make restitution. You are more likely to see restitution or some attempt at restitution made if he is trying to come back to Christ.

Trying to bring about justice is too close to revenge for any of us to walk that line. Absalom tried this and it backfired, causing him to fall. Our courts system (earthly speaking) and God (heavenly speaking) are the only ones ordained to bring about justice. If someone committed a crime, they ought to pay whatever justice the courts deem. It is not our place to impose it, however. It is our job to restore the Fallen Christian.

The victim needs a different type of restoration and healing. Someone does need to help the victim, reach out to the victim, and help the victim to heal. However, the same person can't reach out to both the victim and the Fallen Christian. This only creates confusion and conflict. I'm not even sure you can prioritize between the two. You should help the one you are more capable of helping. Someone else will need to reach out to the other one.

Question: In trying to restore a fallen leader, how do I help him through all the personal attacks by angry followers and other leaders who resent him or feel they can gobble up some of his territory so to speak?

Answer: You won't be able to stop all the attacks. Don't even pretend you can. The best thing you can do is to simply be an anchor that is not attacking, is not demeaning, is not destructive in his life. Always point him to his Saviour, Jesus Christ.

Moses suffered attacks for taking an Ethiopian woman as his wife—something he should not have done. In fact, his own sister and brother attacked him. God, however, defended him (Numbers 12). That is all someone who is under attack needs… someone to defend him.

This does not mean that you defend the wrong, but it does mean that you defend what he did right and is trying to do right. This is the best thing you can do for such a person.

Question: What do I do if my efforts to help a Fallen Christian bring me into conflict with someone else I love?

Answer: This does happen. Sometimes a spouse may feel left out or may feel you are hypocritical because you don't show the same patience or love to your own family. Fellow church members may resent your efforts or feel your efforts are for nothing. Barnabas most likely discovered this problem when he set out to help Paul. Yet his reputation was such that it appears he overcame this problem. He had a good reputation.

You may have to ensure the home front is secure before you venture out to battle. Your influence is severely limited if the people you count on to support you don't. If you find yourself in this position, you may need to refocus your efforts and find someone else to help restore the Fallen Christian. If that is not feasible, you may be forced to slow things down some.

Recall the device Joshua used to win a battle in the book of Joshua. He lured the men away from their homes and sent a second force to burn the city. When the men looked back and saw their homes burning, they immediately feared for their wives and children and suddenly became powerless even to flee (Joshua 8:20). Keep the home front secure!

Question: Is there a point where you just give up on helping someone?

Answer: Being a Restorer can be very taxing on you emotionally and spiritually. It is very disturbing to see someone you are trying to help return to their folly over and over again despite your best efforts. You will want to quit at times.

However, there are only three conditions that will cause me to give up on helping someone. The first is when he refuses my help. You can't help someone who doesn't want your help.

The second reason I would give up is if I lost the heart of the person I am trying to help and have no more influence. The two reasons are close in nature, but they do have subtle nuances in their differences. The second one I may be able to successfully pass on to someone who can capture his heart. The first individual will be resistant to everything and everyone.

The third reason I may quit on someone is if I feel my efforts and help are causing more harm than good. If I am powerless, for example, to make any impact or my efforts create more problems for the individual I am trying to help, I will stop.

I won't give up on someone for any other reason—even if I want to.

Question: I've been trying to restore someone, but every time I try, I get burned. I'm burned out and angry. Should I continue trying to restore this Christian?

Answer: This is closely related to the previous question but with a subtle difference. In this case, you are the one who is hurt. Let me say very clearly that you cannot help anyone when you are injured emotionally or spiritually. You must be strong enough to help. If you are angry, resentful, or depressed, then you are the Fallen Christian in need of restoration. Get help. Pass this individual on to someone else and take the time to come back to a strong relationship with Jesus Christ.

The Bible is very clear that the Restorer needs to be the strong spiritual one. If that is not you, then get help… for your own sake.

Question: What about church discipline? Doesn't the church have the right—the obligation—to discipline sin within its own ranks?

Answer: This is a very touchy question. The church can be used to try and bring about reconciliation between two Christians who are at odds with each other (Matthew 18). The church also has an obligation to protect its members in two ways: first, from false doctrine, and second, from the destructive and divisive sin that could impact other Christians and pull them away from Christ.

The first can and may be taken care of publicly from the pulpit, but the second one should only ever be dealt with from the pulpit if there is no other choice. If the person has been privately addressed and told to stop creating division, but refuses, then the issue may need to be addressed from the pulpit for the sake of church unity and the cause of Christ.

Other than that, I don't think that it is the church's duty or responsibility to publicly flog a Christian for a sin. A church can relieve a Fallen Christian of responsibility—and should—but that is as far as it should go.

Question: What do I do if the Fallen Christian I wish to help doesn't seem to fit any of the types you list in this book?

Answer: Search the Scriptures. This book is not meant to be a replacement for the Word of God. It is meant to point you to the various Scriptures that can help you restore a Fallen Christian. The answers lie in the pages of your Bible. Seek them out.

About the Author

Greg S. Baker was born in 1975 to a Christian couple. Reared in church all his life, he came to accept Jesus as his Saviour and attended a Bible college, graduating with a bachelor's degree in pastoral theology. He pastored a church in northern Colorado for thirteen years until God called him to expand his writing ministry. He now resides in Arizona.

His writing passion pervades nearly every aspect of his life. As a child, he was an avid reader and fell in love with words and their ability to stir the imagination and convey ideas. While in high school, he attempted and completed his first novel only to see it rejected. Despite this setback, he turned his writing skills toward more productive means. It became a tool by which he conveyed his passion for his God and Saviour to the world around him. As a pastor, he used his love for writing to bring to others over twenty years of experience in the ministry, counseling marriages, and healing relationships.

He is married to the love of his life, Liberty, and has six incredible boys who alternately remind him of the excitement of youth and the inevitability of the passage of time. He loves to play sports, play chess, and tinker around with computers. Other than writing, he continues to pastor in various capacities and operates an editing business for Christian authors.